PRAISE FOR
DETERMINED TO

T0145689

"It is my distinct pleasure and privilege to have known and been associated with Leonard Richardson, now Lt. Colonel (Dr.) Leonard Richardson, since his early years spent on the tiny island of Anguilla.

From a very early age Leonard cultivated a broad perspective on life and aspired to achieve the highest and noblest ideals. Fortunately, as he grew in years, the quest for knowledge and experience intensified, and he was adamant that nothing whatsoever would deter him from ascending the highest rung on the ladder of success.

It is therefore not surprising to me that in a short time he accomplished the utmost success in the USAF and in his medical career.

I congratulate him and commend him highly for his book, *Determined to Practice: An Ancient Calling to Provide the Highest Quality of Health Care*. It is my hope that many will benefit immensely from the knowledge contained therein and will be challenged to follow closely in Leonard's footsteps.

It is said that 'Some people are born great, some achieve greatness, and some have greatness thrust upon them.' . . . Leonard's accomplishments accrued from the dint of hard work and submission and obedience to the Spirit of God who guided him over the years."

—Joseph Lloyd (Rev.)

"An inspiring personal story depicting an extraordinary rise from humble beginnings to entrepreneurial success in medicine. It is a must read for anyone who aspires to defy the odds and achieve world-class greatness in business, community, and life."

—Louis G. Hutt, Jr., CPA, Esq.
Author of *The Road to Mega Success: Simple Strategies for Enriching the Bottom Line* and host of *The Lou Hutt Show,* Sirius XM Radio

"In this inspiring account of his determination to practice medicine of the highest quality, Leonard Richardson, MD, captures the challenges in his life and shares with us an inspiring and detailed approach to solving some of today's problems with our health-care system.

Dr. Richardson uses his personal journey and demonstrates how he handled the unpredictable, challenging, and profoundly complex world that is medicine. He embraced technology and weaved together lessons from his childhood, from athletic competition, from a military career, and from civilian medical practice to tell a compelling story of success.

Taking us on a journey that includes thousands of years of his personal legacy, he demonstrates how one's legacy can strengthen one's resolve. He introduces a new model of providing health care and then skillfully pivots toward the future of medicine. He also explains the ingredients necessary for turning today's struggling medical practices into successful enterprises.

It is a breakthrough handbook for surviving and thriving in our complex and ever-shifting world of medicine, and you will want to share this book with everyone you know."

—Edith P. Mitchell, MD, FACP
116th president, National Medical Association

DETERMINED TO
PRACTICE

DETERMINED TO
PRACTICE

AN ANCIENT CALLING TO PROVIDE THE
HIGHEST QUALITY OF HEALTH CARE

LEONARD RICHARDSON, MD

Published by Advantage, Charleston, South Carolina.
Member of Advantage Media Group.

ADVANTAGE is a registered trademark, and the Advantage colophon is a trademark of Advantage Media Group, Inc.

Printed in the United States of America.

Cover Photo by Chris Paulis Photography

ISBN: 978-1-59932-701-3
LCCN: 2016934282

This publication is designed to provide accurate and authoritative information in regard to the subject matter covered. It is sold with the understanding that the publisher is not engaged in rendering legal, accounting, or other professional services. If legal advice or other expert assistance is required, the services of a competent professional person should be sought.

Advantage Media Group is proud to be a part of the Tree Neutral® program. Tree Neutral offsets the number of trees consumed in the production and printing of this book by taking proactive steps such as planting trees in direct proportion to the number of trees used to print books. To learn more about Tree Neutral, please visit **www.treeneutral.com.** To learn more about Advantage's commitment to being a responsible steward of the environment, please visit **www.advantagefamily.com/green**

Advantage Media Group is a publisher of business, self-improvement, and professional development books and online learning. We help entrepreneurs, business leaders, and professionals share their Stories, Passion, and Knowledge to help others Learn & Grow. Do you have a manuscript or book idea that you would like us to consider for publishing? Please visit **advantagefamily.com** or call **1.866.775.1696.**

To my patients:

Thank you for allowing me to be a part of your lives. It has truly been an honor taking care of you through the years, and I have been extremely blessed. I have learned a great deal from you. You have entrusted me with your care from childhood, through your military careers, through your adulthood, and finally, through your later years. I am truly humbled. You will always be part of my family.

Table of Contents

PART 2

FOREWORD

As a former athlete, member of the Royal Air Force, and medical practitioner, I am particularly drawn to the story of this very dynamic and goal-oriented gentleman. So much so that I am moved to pen a few words in honour of his remarkable achievements and worthwhile contributions to his country and fellowmen.

Admittedly, all three disciplines mentioned above have played a significant role in my life, but it is no secret that my heart and soul belong to medicine. My admiration for this profession has been greatly enhanced with the description of the "unspeakable divine" significance of the medical profession as practiced by the contemplative participant in the mystery of life and death—the doctor. Thus, I was thoroughly impressed to learn that Dr. Richardson, from a very tender age, had the wisdom to view his desire to practice medicine as a calling. I glean from his book that Dr. Richardson, like myself, believed and still believes that members of his profession have a solemn and divine obligation—indeed a privilege of the greatest magnitude—to heal, cure, and protect God's greatest miracle: the human being.

However, even beyond the realm of medicine, Dr. Richardson's journey as accounted in his book is both inspirational and empowering. He dared to dream beyond the bounds of the proverbial box, which many of our young West Indian brothers and sisters are confined to. As he put it, "Seek the road less travelled because this is where you will have to be innovative . . ." Undoubtedly, his life and more importantly, his *approach* to life, speaks volumes to what we can all achieve if we are resolute about our passion and the pursuit of it. After all, "You are responsible for your own success. You are in control of your destiny."

Dr. Richardson—athlete, pilot, physician, innovator . . . I salute you. Continue to chase your dreams, to soar above the rest, and to heal the world—body, mind, and spirit.

—Dr. Sir Cuthbert Sebastian, GCMG, OBE, MDCM
Former Governor General for the Federation
of St. Christopher (St. Kitts) and Nevis

ABOUT THE AUTHOR

L t. Colonel (Dr.) Leonard A. Richardson, a flight surgeon, internal-medicine physician, and pilot, attended Howard University College of Medicine from 1989 to 1995 and graduated with an MD degree. Prior to that, he was an undergraduate at Adelphi University in Garden City, New York, from 1987 to 1989 and graduated with a bachelor of science degree.

Dr. Richardson, a native of Anguilla, completed his early school studies before college in St. Kitts, where he proved himself to be an accomplished athlete. He remains the national junior record holder for the 110-meter hurdles and decathlon for St. Kitts and Nevis, and he won a bronze medal in the 1986 decathlon at the Pan-American Junior Athletics Championship.

Upon graduating from Howard University College of Medicine, Dr. Richardson completed a joint internal-medicine residency-training program at Michigan State University, Kalamazoo Center for Medical Studies and at Howard University Hospital. Afterward, he joined the United States Air Force (USAF), where he served with distinction. He graduated at the top of his class from the USAF Officer Training School at Maxwell Air Force Base (AFB) in Alabama, where he was commissioned as a Captain in 1997, after which he obtained his aerospace-medicine certification. He was then stationed at Hill AFB, Utah, where he served as a flight surgeon of the 75th Aerospace Medicine Squadron.

In July 2000, Dr. Richardson returned to civilian life for additional medical training but soon joined the USAF Reserves. He was transferred to Andrews AFB and the 459th Aeromedical Staging Squadron, leading a unit that provided supportive and emergency medical care for war casualties who were transiting the air-evacuation system during operations Nobel Eagle, Enduring Freedom, and Iraqi Freedom. As a civilian, Dr. Richardson worked as an internal-medicine/critical-care unit physician from 2001 to 2011. He is also owner and president of Kingdom Medicine, PA, a private primary-care/internal-medicine practice in Pikesville, Maryland.

As an air force officer, Dr. Richardson was promoted to Major in 2004 and to Lieutenant Colonel in 2012. He served as the chief of aerospace medicine from 2013 to 2016 for the 459th Aerospace Medicine Squadron at Joint Base Andrews.

In January 2013, Lt. Colonel Richardson was selected to lead the USAF Reserve component in the inauguration parade.

Dr. Richardson holds many awards and decorations, which include the Air Force Commendation Medal, with oak leaf cluster; Global War on Terrorism Medal; USAF Achievement Medal; Armed Forces Reserve with Mobilization Medal; USAF Expeditionary Service Ribbon; and an Outstanding Unit citation. He has also served as an FAA aviation medical examiner.

INTRODUCTION

All innovators and dreamers in life have set themselves apart from the pack by not being limited by their surroundings, circumstances, or naysayers. Steve Jobs and Steve Wozniak refused to be limited by their circumstances and surroundings and started their Apple business in the family garage. They funded their entrepreneurial goals by selling their personal items. Fast-forward a few years, and Jobs and Wozniak are now recognized as revolutionaries in the computer industry, making technology accessible to the everyday consumer.

Dr. Charles Drew refused to be limited by the culture of his time, which held that he could not be successful because of the color of his skin, and he became the first African American to graduate from Columbia University Medical School. Dr. Drew then invented a technique to separate and freeze the components of blood so that they could be reconstituted later. This technique saved many, many lives, especially the lives of soldiers during World War II, and continues to do so today through blood banks.

Dr. Charles Drew, Steve Wozniak, and Steve Jobs each reached a place in their lives where they experienced the realization that their dreams had come to fruition. All that they had worked so tirelessly to achieve had happened. They lived to see their dreams become reality.

Many people have experienced a moment like this in their lives. My moment happened while I was on an airplane. (Later in this book, you will learn of the significance of this moment and of my presence on that airplane.)

One day, I was getting a flight to Anguilla, the land of my birth. I had finally come full circle from my childhood upbringing in Anguilla to now flying back there as an adult. During the flight, a quiet moment gave me the opportunity to reflect on my life. This was when I had *my* epiphany: my dreams had finally come true. I wondered how I had gotten to this place in my medical career. How had I managed to accomplish my dream in the face of overwhelming odds? I realized that I hadn't just chosen medicine; in truth, it had chosen me.

How did this little island boy with a big dream get to the point where he had a thriving medical practice in Maryland and was now flying to Anguilla to start up another medical practice? I asked myself, "How did I get here, and how can I preserve this information to pass on to my children?"

This prompted me to figure out how I could capture what I'd learned and applied to my own business success and transfer it to the next generation. The fact is the steps and strategies that I used to get to this place of success can be transferred to any industry; I want every entrepreneur to be able to utilize these same steps and strategies. Initially, I didn't think of capturing my tools for medical-practice success within the pages of a book, but I knew I wanted to pass along some of my wisdom as a keepsake for my son and daughters if they chose to go this route. So, the "pearls" of wisdom contained in this book are my gift to the next generation of life changers, inventors, entrepreneurs, medical geniuses, and other history makers.

I have learned that it is truly beneficial to learn the language of power in order to understand your purpose. In other words, you must understand the rules, governance, and legislature of whatever "landscape" you want to enter to set yourself apart and achieve the success you seek. For me, the language of power was English because, at the time, I was living in a British territory. I needed to be fluent in English in order to be understood and, in turn, be able to excel in whatever I was doing at school and work. However, if I had grown up in Guadeloupe or Paris, then French would have been my language of power. It is important to understand the environment, the "landscape" where you live. This is key to being successful.

How can medical professionals successfully understand their environment and learn to speak the language needed to succeed in their practice? Hopefully, that is what you will learn through the pages of this book as I introduce my business model. In addition, you will also understand the importance of passion and the pursuit of it. Moreover, I advise you to seek the road less traveled because this is where you have to be innovative and where your entrepreneurial spirit will be stroked.

So what makes my business success model different from other business success models? The truth is that it's not absolutely new. It's a concept I have adopted by simply observing and recognizing what I have learned from others, including what my father taught me about success when I was young and impressionable. I didn't fully understand it then, but through his lessons, he was actually providing me with the tools I would need to succeed in every new season of my life. Even though my father passed away when I was twenty-four years of age, by then, his words of wisdom were already instilled in my brain.

This book will explain how my work experiences in both a hospital and a private medical practice helped me discover—or rediscover—how to practice traditional medicine as part of a profitable business model that can be replicated by others who dream of achieving autonomous business success. Once it is more widely adopted, this model will allow me, in partnership with other doctors, to expand my resources to bring the very best patient care to everyone who needs it.

I hope that my words will teach, motivate, encourage, and inspire doctors to be entrepreneurs in their own businesses. You will notice that at the end of each chapter I've written a "pearl" of wisdom for you to ponder, and eventually apply, as you reflect on the lessons I have learned and am now sharing with you.

Everyone has a personal journey to travel. I had to find mine, and you will have to find yours. You will have to decide if you want to do better than the circumstances you were dealt. If you want to do something different with your life, and if you don't know how, I urge you to look within and use the tools available to you—some of which you will learn from this book—and the passions that you must awaken within your spirit in order to get to that place of success.

PART 1

LESSONS FROM MY PAST

Early family photograph.
From left to right, Paulette Richardson, Leonard Richardson, Constantine Richardson, Dulcie Richardson, Dawn Richardson. (baby)
Photographer: Vincent Inniss

CHAPTER 1

GROWING UP IN ANGUILLA AND ST. KITTS

Life is a succession of lessons which must be lived to be understood.
—Helen Keller

I can honestly say that I had a wonderful childhood growing up in Anguilla, a small island in the Lesser Antilles, which are in the West Indies. Anguilla is one of the many islands in the Caribbean that has been labeled a paradise. It has also enjoyed a reputation as "the culinary capital of the Caribbean" because of its variety of cuisines featuring native Caribbean, Spanish, French, African, and English cuisines. I was

Photograph by Leonard Richardson M.D.
View of Sandy Ground, Anguilla

born in Anguilla in 1967 and also lived for other parts of the year on the neighboring island of St. Kitts. I was my parents' first son and the second of their five children. When I was young, the small islands of St. Kitts and Anguilla were engaged in a dispute over resources and

View of Basseterre, St. Kitts
Photographer: Leonard Richardson, MD

self-determination. Anguilla wanted to secede from the Federation of St. Kitts, Nevis, and Anguilla. St. Kitts wanted its independence from Great

Britain, and Anguilla wanted to remain under British rule. The amphibious assault by the 2nd Battalion Parachute Regiment, code name Operation Sheepskin, occurred when British paratroopers invaded Anguilla to quell the rebellion, but

B company 2nd Battalion Parachute Regiment leave Anguilla for Britain on an Andover aircraft. Source: paradata.org.uk

not a shot was fired. It was dubbed the "world's smallest revolution." Anguilla ended up remaining under British rule while St. Kitts and Nevis eventually gained their independence.

My parents, both teachers working for the government of St. Kitts, Nevis, and Anguilla at the time, ended up leaving Anguilla to

Home of my birth and early Childhood.
Built by my Great-Grandfather, Morsa Brooks.
Photographer: Leonard Richardson M.D.

live in St. Kitts. So I was sort of Anguillan but began living in St. Kitts because of my parents' occupations. I traveled back and forth to Anguilla during my early years, visiting my grandparents. During this time, I had an opportunity to see how my parents grew up when they first lived in Anguilla.

The time I spent with my grandparents was humbling. We had outdoor latrines and no running water or electricity. We had kerosene lamps, did our laundry outside with washboards, and drank our water from a cistern. I was very young, but I still remember it vividly. When I went back to St. Kitts to be with my parents, I would experience a different life. I remember my parents working two jobs, buying and building their first home, and buying their first car, and I remember our first television set. *Sesame Street* was the first show I watched. Experiencing these two extremes in my childhood helped to shape my life for the better and teach me the value of what I had.

In our culture, my parents' lives were seen by many as a success model. My parents began with a humble life in Anguilla, but they wanted better for all of us, so they worked hard to achieve it. I witnessed them work hard and become successful in that society through their pursuit of higher education. They demonstrated success by their example.

One of my fondest memories of living in Anguilla and St. Kitts is of going to the beach on a Saturday morning with a few of the neighborhood children to walk, watch the sunrise, swim, and train for sports day. Who doesn't love the

Rendezvous Bay, Anguilla
Photographer: Leonard Richardson M.D.

beach? We would run on the sand because its resistance helped to make our muscles stronger in preparation for running on the track, when the time came. I loved sports as I was growing up. My friends and I would also chase each other and swim. Saturday was the best day of the week for us: no school and no worries.

Another fond memory I have of growing up in Anguilla and St. Kitts is that of going to the airport. My family and I would always go to the airport to welcome arriving family members or send off departing family members. Incidentally, we also got to see many other people coming to and going from Anguilla and St. Kitts. These beautiful islands in the Caribbean have always attracted many tourists. For the most part, at that time, the airplanes that flew in to the Anguillian airport were small, but when they extended the airport in St. Kitts to raise it to international status, large airplanes began landing. Internationalizing the airport was a grand event. Television cameras were there to record it. When more visitors and large jets started coming in, what also came with these large jets were small private jets. Getting off these airplanes were people I'd never seen before: wealthy individuals who would fly to our island for a few days and spend in one night what would have taken my father one year to make.

Robert L. Bradshaw International Airport
Photographer: Leonard Richardson, MD

These were people with tremendous means, and seeing them made me question what I wanted my future to look like. I had never despised my humble beginnings in life, but my goals for success included having a future that did not look like my humble beginnings. I wanted more of what the world had to offer; I dreamed of more. When I asked my father about this, he told me that there was another world out there, far from my humble beginnings. He pointed at a jet and said, "When you come back here (one day), you're going to be like them, and you're going to own that." Those words stuck with me for my entire life because he was, basically, telling me that I had endless possibilities.

Parents want their children's successes in life to be bigger than their successes. They dream for their children a better future than the life they have, which is why my mother and father pushed my siblings and me to success. They challenged us to dream of success and to make a plan to achieve it.

My father's own success came through education. He was an intellectual. He studied at the University of the West Indies and completed a master's degree in history at the University of Alberta in Canada. In addition, my father was a dean, or resident tutor, as it is now called, for the University of the West Indies. He also wrote a book titled *The United States and Argentina, 1945–1947: A Case Study in Diplomatic Practice.*

Growing up, I'd always ask my father questions about anything and everything. I would challenge him with my questions because he was a historian. He understood Western history and European history, but when he couldn't answer my questions, he

Photograph of Constantine Richardson's book.
Photographer: Leonard Richardson M.D.

would deflect back to me. Once, I asked him where our ancestors had come from, and his answer was, "You have to find that out." Although he didn't always answer my numerous questions, he always challenged me to find out more on my own.

In fact, one of the reasons I think my brother and I write is because our father was our mentor, and he led by example. Unfortunately, as I mentioned earlier, my father passed away when I was twenty-four years old.

My mother has also been a great example in my life and is still alive. She lives with me for about half of the year until it gets cold, and she also goes to the homes of my other siblings. She still has her own home in St. Kitts and spends the winter there.

She is retired now, after dedicating years of service to teaching and serving. Her legacy of success includes being an officer of the

Investiture of Dulcie Elaine Richardson, OBE
at Buckingham Palace.
Photographer: Charles Green photography

British Empire and being awarded a medal by Queen Elizabeth II at Buckingham Palace. She was also an educator in Anguilla. She trained others to be teachers in St. Kitts at the Teacher's Training College which later became the College of Further Education, as their Principal. Both my mother and father were instrumental in education. In fact, after going to St. Kitts and being trained in education and getting their appropriate certificates, one of the things my parents did when they returned to Anguilla was to become foundation members of the first high school in Anguilla. They became leaders in the society and influenced many to follow the road toward a successful life. They were visionaries.

Even with his prestigious academic degree, I think my father recognized that he had some limitations. He didn't know how I should obtain that jet, but he knew how to give me the tools to figure it out. My father taught me, based on how he viewed success, and I valued the lessons I learned from him. However, I wanted to challenge his success model. When I saw other people coming to the Caribbean on their expensive jets and spending their money, enjoying themselves at our beaches, in our restaurants, and in our taxis, I noticed that what they spent on leisure would have been the means to survive for many of the folks I grew up with. I could not reconcile myself to this disparity.

For instance, tourists rode around on ATVs or their yachts, and I saw luxury that my family could not possibly afford. As a result, I started to think we might not be as successful as I had believed.

I thought that my family was rich because we had a car and a home, and my siblings and I were doing well in school. Those were the elements of success. We were all taught that if you worked hard, got good school grades, got a good job, and you made a good living, you would be happy and successful. This was the measure of success we used because it was all we knew. However when I saw those people living their luxurious lifestyle, I realized that I could work for fifty years and would never be able to spend what they were spending in one week.

Growing up, I had everything I needed, and I loved my childhood. I embraced the situation my family was in when I was young, and I never looked down on them because of it. Nonetheless, I also recognized that I needed (and wanted) to do more. There was another side to this coin, and I didn't reject it at all. I wanted and needed to dream of a different world from the one I grew up in and a different kind of success from what my parents had achieved. I began to realize, even at a young age, that when I grew up, I couldn't just work for somebody; I needed to figure out how I could be the employer. Now, the success model that I have followed in my life marries the lessons of education and hard work, coupled with entrepreneurship and owning my own business.

The measure of success for one person will not look the same as the measure of success for another. For those tourists who traveled to and from Anguilla and St. Kitts in their private jets, spending thousands of dollars on their vacations, their material possessions, and their jet-setting lifestyle was the epitome of success. On the other hand, my idea of success entailed more than vacations and nice things; my success encompassed my career and dreams of a better life.

When I asked my father why the tourists were able to live such extravagant lives that were so different from our own, he answered, "You have to go and figure this out. I've given you the tools that I can, but you have to take it to the next level."

And so I did.

PEARL #1:

You are responsible for your own success.
You are in control of your destiny.

CHAPTER 2

EARLY ACCOMPLISHMENTS AND THE USAF

A dream doesn't become reality through magic.
It takes sweat, determination, and hard work.
—Colin Powell

I always knew what I wanted to be. As early as age six, I had no other dream but to become a pilot and a doctor. These two professions joined my love of flying with my love of medicine. I also knew that I would go to the United States to study. At first, my parents didn't understand why I wanted to study in the United States. They lived in a British territory, so their thought was always that their children would go to the University of the West Indies, get a first degree, and then go to England and get their masters degree or a medical degree. My medical degree would then bring me back home to work in the hospital. This was my parents' traditional way of seeing how things needed to be done.

But I didn't want to do things the traditional way; I wanted to really figure out the world for myself. I wanted to see the world, and I wanted to do it all. When my parents finally acknowledged that my dream to live and study in the United States would never disappear, they knew I needed to leave St. Kitts and Anguilla and find success on my own terms. They told me, "We can't afford to send you to an American college. We can only afford one semester." So I made a deal with them. "Okay," I said, "pay for one semester, and I'll find a way to get the rest." They agreed and cleaned out their bank account to give me the money. This was incredibly difficult for them to do because it wasn't just about me; they had four other children to take care of. My parents knew, however, that in Anguilla and St. Kitts, opportunities were limited if you didn't have money and an advanced education, which most folks didn't have. They knew that given my personality, there would be better opportunities for me in the United States or another developed country.

There were a few people with the right finances who could send their kids off to study in the United States, Canada, or England, but the majority of the population in St. Kitts and Anguilla couldn't afford to do that. The only person without wealth who got the opportunity to go away to study was the state scholar. If you were the state scholar, then the government would pay for you to go off and study something that the government officials thought their country would need.

Well, I wasn't the state scholar; I was in the top five, but I wasn't number one. My dad would always tell me, "It's not that they're smarter than you. They just work harder than you." This pushed me to seriously think about how I could work harder at my other talents.

This was when I focused on what I was really good at, which was running. I was a part of the track team for many years, and it was something I really enjoyed doing. I figured out that running was an ability I had, and I needed to stand out from the other athletes so that I could earn a scholarship to attend a university in the United States.

Back then, no one received track scholarships or sporting scholarships. The majority of scholarships were for academics. You had to be good in physics, chemistry, biology, and mathematics. Those students would get the state scholarship to attend a university and study what the government required, based on whatever professional skill was in high demand for the island. Therefore, my only choice was to find another way to get a scholarship, and that's what I did.

CHASING MY DREAM

Let me first speak of how I developed this love for running and how it led me to receive a scholarship. In the Caribbean, you realize pretty early if you have a knack for running or not. In primary school, everyone is put out on a line and the teachers have you run. In St. Kitts and Anguilla, a student's sports choices are limited to just a few: cricket, soccer, and track and field. I realized early that I had the ability to run. After choosing your sport in school, you get an opportunity to compete in your local sports day, and if you are one of the better athletes, you are chosen to compete in the biggest school competition, the interschool sports. We competed against other schools, and those who showed promising ability were selected, along with the best athletes in the country, to compete against other Caribbean countries.

This was when I started realizing that in other countries, the ability to run could sometimes lead to scholarships for college. This could be a way for me to get out of St. Kitts or Anguilla, earn a scholarship, and get into college. What I needed was to be seen on the world stage. To do this, I had to be chosen from my school. By this time, I was in high school, and I had to be chosen for the national team, which meant I had to be the best in high school. I then had to be the best in the country, once all the schools had competed, and after that, I would get a chance to go to the CARIFTA Games (the Caribbean Free Trade Association's national championships). After learning of these games, I started training to prepare myself to win.

I trained rigorously. I would run in the mountains in the morning, starting at five AM. I would also run on the beach, in the sand, as hard as I could because I had to beat the current high-school champion, Joel Herbert. Joel Herbert was the best, and he didn't lose. I chose a middle-distance race—the eight hundred-meter race— because I wasn't the fastest but had some endurance.

In the finals of my high school's eight hundred-meter race, I was able to beat Joel. It was the hardest race that I ever had to run. Despite this fact, I wasn't chosen for the national team to attend the CARIFTA Games because the national team student had to be chosen ahead of time by the committee. That student had to show overall excellence in all of the other races leading up to the national championship. Joel had such a great reputation that they chose him for the team in advance; they had put him on the list even before I beat him in the Basseterre High School eight hundred-meter finals. Basically, he already had his one-way ticket to the CARIFTA Games. I had no ill feelings toward Joel. In fact, I truly admired his athletic ability. It still hurt, however, that I had not been chosen to represent the country.

Not getting a chance to go to the CARIFTA Games was, of course, very disappointing. However, it wasn't over for me at that point. All the qualified individuals who were on the St. Kitts track team for the CARIFTA Games (athletes under twenty years of age) were also invited to the Pan-American Junior Athletics Championship to be held in Winter Park, Florida, in 1986. Twenty-five nations were represented there. The trip could not be financed by the St. Kitts/Nevis amateur athletics association because of a lack of funding, so the invitation was, initially, declined. When I heard about the invitation, I petitioned the St. Kitts/Nevis amateur athletics association to be allowed to participate and was given the opportunity to represent the country, provided I could pay my own way. I immediately started washing cars to raise funds. This was the national audience I needed for the chance to be offered a track scholarship.

When my parents saw that I was really working at this, and people were giving small donations to my fundraiser, they realized that I was serious. Overall, I think I had to raise about $1,300 from private donations and washing cars, and my parents kicked in the rest. So that's how I got to the Pan-American games. Once there, I competed in the decathlon, which involved ten different events. This was my very first time competing in all of these events. I was learning the decathlon while I was doing it. Crazy, right? But I knew I had convinced people to invest in me, so I had no choice but to do my best to succeed. I didn't want to let them and myself down.

I knew I had some running ability, but I hadn't been trained in some of the field events. I was scared, but at the same time, I was grateful for the opportunity to showcase my talents. While other athletes were warming up, I focused on what they were doing and imitated them so I could learn their techniques. This was the only time I had to gain some level of understanding of the events in which

I was about to compete. I was eager to impress the coaches who could possibly offer me a scholarship.

My first event was the one hundred meters, followed by the long jump, the high jump, shot put, pole vault, 110-meter hurdles, discus, javelin, four hundred meters, and finally, the 1,500 meters. I still remember the athletes. One was Miguel Valle, a gold medalist from Cuba and the Cuban decathlon champion. Emilio Valle, his brother, was the 110-meters hurdles champion and also the four hundred-meters hurdles champion. It was Miguel Valle who eventually won the decathlon, and in second place was Shawn Collins from the United States. At that time, no one knew that while I was competing in these events, I was also learning the techniques. Miguel Valle realized I didn't have prior knowledge and was learning the techniques as I went along. I remember him whispering to me in Spanish, and the translator would translate quietly. He would give me coaching lessons during the event, with advice such as, "You need to lengthen your run up," or "You need to shorten your run up." I was confident about the running events but not confident about the field events. I'm grateful to Miguel Valle for those lessons.

The person I had to beat out for third place was Richard Beatty,

the reigning American Junior Olympics decathlon champion. It was intimidating, but I did beat Richard Beatty that year and won a bronze medal. This was the first medal for St. Kitts in an international competition. In addition, I set the record for the pole vault and 110 hurdles. (I still hold that record, thirty years later, in the national junior decathlon.) I think it's the longest-standing record for St. Kitts. This became a historic

Pan American Junior Games bronze medal. Photographer: Leonard Richardson M.D.

occasion. The games were televised in Florida and made newspaper headlines in St. Kitts and Anguilla as well.

Just as I had learned valuable lessons in achieving success from my father, I also learned valuable lessons in success from Miguel Valle at the Pan-American Games. At any stage of life, you must always value what those who have gone before you teach you.

I had persevered on my journey. My performance in track and field led to a scholarship that would allow me to leave St. Kitts and Anguilla for America. I was on the path to achieve my ultimate goal of becoming a physician.

Although I knew that I wanted to attend college, I also had a strong desire to join the air force. My scholarship would not completely fund my education, and I realized that by joining the air force, I could use the GI Bill or some form of tuition reimbursement to help pay for college. I knew immediately that I wanted to be an officer because I intended to be a physician. So I couldn't enlist in the air force first if I wanted to become an officer. For that, I would need to at least get into medical school before joining the air force. I completed my undergraduate studies in two and a half years because the track team was cancelled while I was an undergraduate, so my track scholarship would run out, leaving me without any funds for the remainder of my education.

I completed thirty credits each semester and an additional twelve credits during the summer session. I worked really hard to get as many credits as I could out of the way while applying early to medical school. For my undergraduate degree, I attended Adelphi University on Long Island, New York. Then I attended Howard University College of Medicine in Washington, DC, where I enjoyed being part of a large international student population.

THE USAF

Still thinking about my dream to be an officer in the United States Air Force (USAF), I applied for the air force while I was in medical school. My dream to be a physician had not been deferred, but I wanted to ensure that I would find a way to join the air force and get my medical degree paid for. At the time, the air force had a Health Profession Services Program (HPSP) in which, if you committed to the USAF, you would receive additional monies for medical-school training and residency. In return, when you were finished, you would owe the air force the same amount of time it took you to complete your training and your residency. This is what I did. Whatever the number of years I would take to complete my medical training, I promised those years back to the air force.

However, even though I signed up for the USAF, the scholarship was not guaranteed; I still needed to earn it. While doing this, I had an opportunity to see which medical fields were available through the air force. When I talked to the recruiters, I realized there was a field called flight medicine, or aerospace medicine, which allowed you to have pilot training to possibly fly jets. Right away, I knew this was exactly what I wanted to do. All bets were off at that point. I had found my calling, and I was going to pursue it with all my might.

Initially, when I first pursued my dream of becoming a physician and began medical school, my goal was to do internal medicine. However, when I learned about the aerospace-medicine program, I switched gears and focused on getting into that program. At the same time, I graduated from Howard Medical School and was accepted into an internal-medicine residency-training program, but I chose to leave that residency early to go into aerospace medicine because a slot opened up. The way it works in the military is that if a slot opens up, you take it immediately because you don't know when another one might become available. The military trains you in what it needs, not what you want. So I seized the opportunity. I dove right into the program without hesitation.

Since I had already graduated from medical school, I was a general medical officer, but I wasn't specialized. Normally, medical-school graduates complete their residency, which determines what their specialty, or focus, will be. However, I postponed my residency and jumped at the chance to join the aerospace-medicine program. When I was stationed, I tested out for high-performance aircraft and ended up going to Hill Air Force Base and being assigned to an F-16 fighter squadron.

Captain Richardson with an F-16 Fighting Falcon. Photographer: 514th Flight Test Squadron pilot

Allow me to explain a little about what exactly flight medicine—or aerospace medicine—is.

One of a doctor's roles in aerospace medicine is to understand the environment pilots work in because the pilots are the patients. We aerospace-medicine doctors have to make sure that pilots are fit,

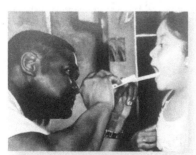

Lt. Col. Leonard Richardson examines a young patient during a humanitarian operation. Source: Air Force Art Collection, Pentagon; oil on canvas by Christopher Hopkins

ready to fly, fight, and win. We experience what they experience, which makes the training very intense.

Sometimes, your success journey requires that you walk in the shoes of those who will need your help.

Another of a doctor's roles in aerospace medicine concerns humanitarian missions. One mission

I was assigned to was in South America, where we went to disadvantaged villages and provided medical care to people who needed it.

A third role of doctors in the USAF aerospace-medicine program is caring for wounded soldiers in flight and getting the injured back to the United States.

The military's aerospace-medicine program involves travel to foreign places, and this, sometimes, requires a lot of physical activity. Physical activity was not something I feared, but the physical *and* emotional toll was on a different level. This was war. The simple, focused athletic training that I had done with the track team would not even come close to the broad training I received in the air force. The pilots, astronauts, air crews, special forces, and missile crews of the air force work under stressors and conditions nobody else in the world experiences. These unique airmen require unique primary care, preventive medicine, and occupational medicine. Flight surgeons have a multitude of responsibilities, some of which include:

- providing medical support to the line (commissioned officers in the USAF who exercise general command authority and hold operational command positions as opposed to officers who normally exercise authority within a specialty), including duty in all aspects of special operations

- determining fitness for flying and special operations duties

- providing medical care for aircrews and missile crews

- evaluating living and working conditions to detect and control health hazards

- participating regularly in flying missions (of nearly all types of aircraft platform) to observe and advise on aeromedical issues

- developing and managing preventive medicine programs, including the education of flight personnel in healthy lifestyles

- establishing procedures for managing casualties in aviation accidents and other disasters

- providing advice on aeromedical evacuation and serving on aviation mishap investigation boards

- serving as the liaison between flying squadrons and medical services

Aerospace medicine primary training includes aeromedical topics, aircrew and survival training, and, of course, rigorous physical training.

A TIME TO REMEMBER

My most memorable experience in the air force was flying at twice the speed of sound over the snow-capped Rocky Mountains in Utah and Colorado. A significant amount of testing occurs in training to make sure you are qualified. However, when you're strapping the jet on, your parachute is in the ejection seat and primed, the canopy is coming down, and your mask is on, you simply hope that you are actually prepared for what's about to happen. When you take off, the jet engines slam you back in your seat as you hurtle down the runway, and then you zoom straight up, instantly, to ten thousand feet. When you are overlooking Salt Lake City or peering out at the beautiful snow-capped Rocky Mountains, there's no other rush quite like it. Nothing in the world can compare to that feeling.

Other memories from my time in the air force include the work during Operation Iraqi Freedom. I remember looking at an airplane filled with wounded soldiers during the early part of the war. Sometimes, our aircraft went out and picked wounded soldiers up. Sometimes, we were in a contingency aeromedical staging facility (CASF), a temporary facility for prepping and staging war casualties for transport. These facilities are usually on the flight line or associated with a hospital that provides critical "stable care" in the hospital's battlefield-care process. Patients who arrived in a stabilized condition from the battlefield were transferred to the CASF while awaiting a flight to a medical center outside the war zone. Oftentimes, we transported them from Baghdad to Kuwait, and from Kuwait to Germany, where they could get secondary-level care.

Imagine this scene: We are on a mission, flying into a war zone, and the lights of the plane are turned off. As we get closer and closer to the zone, the plane begins to spiral down. When we look out the windows of the plane, we see gunfire coming at us. Surprisingly, everyone is calm, fully prepared for the assumed mayhem we are about to jump into. Even when I was flying through dark war zones with gunfire around me, interestingly enough, I was never scared. I never felt I didn't need to be there.

Sometimes, these missions were long and arduous for both service members and military families. Some of my colleagues even experienced mental collapse due to stress and absence from their families. The effect of war can extend far beyond the deployed service member. Families may struggle with the absence of a parent/spouse—something I have experienced personally. So when you show up with your unit at the deployed location's airport and you see an airplane marked "USAF," knowing you're going home is a great feeling.

The air force was always where I knew I belonged. In fact, one of the most impressive things that I've had the opportunity to be a part of was a result of my being chosen to lead the USAF Reserves for the 2012 presidential inauguration. I had the privilege to salute the president of the United States, and it is a day I will never forget.

I experienced many joyous moments in the USAF, as well as hardships.

In life, we may encounter unforeseen challenges. However, if we have prepared well and are intent on seeing our dreams become a reality, we can confidently handle any circumstance.

PEARL #2:

There's no progress without action. Be proactive, perceive it, believe it, do it.

CHAPTER 3

EARNING MY MD

Wherever the art of medicine is loved, there is love of humanity.
—Hippocrates

The air force was a stepping-stone to completing medical school and enabling me to earn my medical certification in aerospace medicine. After serving full-time in the air force, I went back to finishing my specialty in internal medicine. I started internal-medicine studies at Michigan State University and did the first two years there. I completed my third year at Howard University Hospital, where I completed my residency in internal medicine. Howard University College of Medicine was founded in 1868 and has a long and illustrious history of "training students to become competent and compassionate physicians who provide health care in medically underserved communities." The college places strong emphasis on training students to become public health professionals and doctors in underserved communities. Howard University College of Medicine has produced—and continues to produce—a significant number of the nation's top minority physicians, having the "largest concentration of black faculty and student scholars in the country." This was my alma mater, my standard of excellence in medicine. I was proud to see this success happen for me and proud to be a part of such a successful legacy.

I began my residency at Michigan State University's Kalamazoo Center for Medical Studies. Unfortunately, I experienced quite a bit of discrimination while I was there and lost interest in the residency training program. When I first started my residency, nobody looked like me. So it could be very disheartening to walk into a room and be the only African American there. For the most part, my patients loved me, and they enjoyed interacting with me. However, on occasion, I would meet patients who would stare at me in horror and refuse to let me touch them. I learned to smile and say, "I want you to be comfortable, so let's find somebody you're more comfortable with." Even though I learned to put on a smile, my emotions ripped through my body like a knife when this happened.

Eventually, I transferred to Washington, DC, so that I could join a more diverse population of doctors. A larger number of doctors in Washington, DC, were African Americans, and on occasion, I would find myself reaching out to other doctors who had similar experiences to mine. I also learned about and joined the National Medical Association (NMA), which was comprised of a group of physicians who formed this association because African American physicians were not allowed to join the American Medical Association at that time. The NMA is an organization with a history of providing support and opportunities for African American doctors. The NMA mission is dedicated to "advance the art and science of medicine for people of African descent through education, advocacy, and health policy, promoting health and wellness, eliminating health disparities, and sustaining physician viability."

Our association meetings provided a place where doctors would get together to share ideas and make changes that promoted health and wellness, especially within minority communities and populations. We were all attempting to figure it out together, and we were not always ahead of the curve. Sometimes, we received information late, such as access to research data, participation in research studies, continuing medical education, and being included in health-care-policy decision making. Our mutual struggle was that we were all trying to keep the lights on because medicine is a very competitive environment. But our times together were a place to find solace.

I must note that discrimination no longer exists in the American Medical Association. On July 10, 2008, the American Medical Association, the nation's largest organization of physicians, apologized for its history of discriminatory policies toward African American physicians. These policies of discrimination have contributed to disparity in health care for African Americans and have led to a decline in the health of African Americans when compared to their white counterparts.

RESIDENCY TRAINING

Residency was empowering for me because I was now a physician in name and no longer just studying to be one. However, I was also apprehensive about my residency because I was still learning. And, as is any residency program in medicine, it was grueling. Medical residency training begins after graduating from an accredited medical school with a medical degree. In the United States, medical residency training is required to practice medicine in a hospital or in a private practice. Once your residency training is complete, you become board certified by the American Board of Specialties. A residency-training program usually lasts for a minimum of three years for primary-care physicians and up to five years for some surgical specialties.

Medical residency is like an apprenticeship program in which you're being trained by attending physicians. In the 1990s, the number of patients to which you were assigned was unlimited, as was how long you stayed up, so it turned into a hazing process of sorts for new residents.

Residents are now, by law, only allowed to practice or to see patients during a certain period of time, and then they must take a break, and they can be assigned only a certain number of patients. When I was in residency, we didn't have any of these perks, and hazing was a rite of passage. Everybody went through the brutal side of medical residency, and it was tough. But that's how you learned. You learned to function with a lack of sleep and working long hours for days at a time.

No matter how tough the residency program was, you just had to persevere and hope that once you got through it, you would never have to work that hard again. I was motivated because no matter what, I knew I wanted to be a doctor. I had set this as a goal a long time before, and I was going to accomplish it no matter the lack of sleep or the hardship.

Alongside the challenges of medical residency, I also experienced many joys. I was now beginning to live the dream. I was now a physician. I was now involved in life-and-death situations. I was now running "code blues" in the hospital where a multitude of medical personnel stood around a bed. I was the one intubating the patient, ordering medications, and putting in central lines. I was also the one giving life—the one demanding "260 joules," or "300," and giving orders to "shock, shock." There's nothing more exciting than that—well, except for flying at Mach Two in an F-16 air force jet.

Then there was the fact that I was actually saving lives! This gave me great personal satisfaction because I knew that my training and hard work had resulted in someone getting another chance at life.

In addition, my family was proud to say that I was now a physician. Becoming a doctor is something that my culture views as a very noble and remarkable achievement. I decided to attend medical school early, initially because of my father, who had become ill during my first year of undergraduate studies. I hastened my journey through medical school so that he could see me earn my medical degree, but unfortunately, he passed away in my final year. When I told my mother about my disappointment, she shared with me something I did not know. "He knew you were graduating," she said. "He was very proud. You only had a few months to go, and he understood that." So it was comforting that my father had seen my journey and was proud of me.

I was very idealistic while I was in my residency—I had a naïve view of what life would be like as a doctor, once I had completed my residency training. I had it all planned out: I would have patients who loved me; I would be financially secure; my loans would be paid off in two or three years; I'd have job security; my colleagues would respect and love me; I would be independent, and I'd have complete autonomy. I assumed doctors would be like the doctors in the Caribbean who were held in high esteem in society and highly respected.

That was the plan I had set for myself. There's nothing wrong with envisioning your future and picturing your dreams coming true. However, you must have a plan in place, or else it's just paper in the wind, dreams passing by.

When my residency was complete, I still held on to my idealistic view of medicine, of medical practice, and of a hospital career. By this time, I had served one tour in the USAF, and I was now ready to join the ranks of attending physicians in the hospital or out in the world. I had finally arrived. It was time to get paid, pay off my debts, and become that person I wanted to be, the kind of wealthy person I used to see visiting the Caribbean when I was a child.

When my residency was complete, I thought that working in the hospital would be the best decision because there was an opportunity to make some money, and the hospitals paid well. Primary-care doctors were not hiring, and this was when I realized that something was amiss in primary care. (But we'll discuss more about primary care in a later chapter.)

Starting a practice wasn't feasible, considering the hundreds of thousands of dollars' worth of medical-school loans to pay back. So it wasn't possible to simply hang a shingle and start seeing patients. Being in the air force was a tremendously rewarding time in my life. However, I still had the responsibility, after medical school, to pay back my school loans. The air force paid a portion of my medical school/residency program, but the one thing I hadn't realized was that when I switched from internal medicine to aerospace medicine, everything changed. My initial contract with the air force was only for internal medicine. Once I switched to aerospace medicine, that contract was broken.

While I was in the air force, they stopped paying my education expenses and informed me that the money I had initially received for medical school would have to be refunded. I contacted the air force representative. "Wait a second," I said. "You said that if I came into a critical specialty, I'd get this money. Aerospace medicine is still a critical specialty."

"Yes, it is a critical specialty," they replied, "but we weren't paying money for that at that time. It's [from] two different budgets."

This left me saddled with paying back the loan I got from the air force, and I also had medical-school loans to pay back. It was at this point that my idealism about practicing medicine started to fade. Nonetheless, I was still grateful for the fact that I had gotten the opportunity to fly and be trained in aerospace medicine. I would have done it all over again the same way. This experience did not leave me with a feeling of ill will against the air force; in fact, I'm still a part of the USAF Reserves. It just left a hole in my pocket.

PEARL #3:
Don't reinvent the wheel. Learn from those who have gone before you.

CHAPTER 4

HOSPITAL CAREER

We look for medicine to be an orderly field of knowledge and procedure, but it is not. It is an imperfect science, an enterprise of constantly changing knowledge, uncertain information, fallible individuals, and at the same time, lives on the line. There is science in what we do, yes, but also habit, intuition, and sometimes plain old guessing. The gap between what we know and what we aim for persists. And this gap complicates everything we do.
—Atul Gawande, *Complications: A Surgeon's Notes on an Imperfect Science*

I had finally reached a prestigious place in my life: I had graduated with my medical degree, trained in the air force, completed my residency training, and was now a fully credentialed internal-medicine physician at the hospital.

I experienced quite a number of joys during my hospital career, and one of the initial joys was my salary. Finally, for the first time, I was making a decent paycheck. In fact, one of the first things that I set out to do when I received my hospital paycheck was to purchase a car. I could, finally, buy a car that was not an old, second-hand, beat-up lemon. I envisioned myself going to the car dealership and saying, "Hey, I'd like that car." Then they would ask, "Well, what do you do?" To which I would reply, "I'm a doctor." After hearing about my profession, they would then tell me what type of car I would qualify for.

In addition to being able to purchase a reliable and nice-looking car for the first time, I was now able to buy myself a home. So I bought a little townhouse. When you realize that you are in a profession in which you don't have to scrape by any longer but can afford some of the finer things in life, it certainly brings you joy. I thought that I had finally arrived.

My joys also centered around the fact that I now had enough money to start paying off my medical-school loans. There's nothing like the confidence you feel when you have the ability to pay off your debts and have financial security while living your childhood dream all at the same time. To top it off, the biggest joy in becoming a fully credentialed doctor and having a hospital career was that I was now seasoned in the knowledge of medicine. All of those years of learning and training had finally culminated in working in a hospital alongside other doctors. I was not just learning anymore, and I was no longer hesitant to practice medicine on patients. I didn't have to wonder if what I was doing was correct. Confidence now took the lead, and I walked right beside it. I now knew what I was doing and had become one of the masters in the field—if you can say that anyone is truly a master at anything. It was both humbling and satisfying at the same time.

THE CHALLENGES

Initially, it seemed I had some autonomy and job security. However, things soon started to change. With any set of joys, there is also a set of challenges. I would say that when I first began my hospital career, time became my biggest challenge. There was not enough time to complete my work, not enough time to sleep, and extensive time away from my family—more than I liked. I realized that as hard as I was working, I still needed to work harder, putting in lots of hours almost every day of the week in order to stand out to my superiors. I thought I would have time to do everything I could possibly want to do: I'd be able to travel. I'd be able to have dispensable income. I'd be able to pay my medical-school loans off in three years. I had high hopes, but it didn't quite happen that way.

I was making my medical-school loan payments, but I was also working intensely long hours to do it. Let me paint a picture for you of a typical day in the life of a hospitalist, also known as a doctor in a hospital. A typical day involved an initial sign out from the previous physician on call, floor rounds on twenty to thirty patients, ER admissions and hospital discharges, family meetings, codes, central lines, intubations and crisis management, dictating and completing medical records and reviewing charts, communicating with community attending physicians and, eventually, signing out to the incoming physician. This usually lasted twelve to fourteen hours per day, and then you would prepare to do it all over again for the next shift. Days ranged from calm and orderly to highly intense and completely chaotic. The beauty was that my job was to bring order out of this chaos. Calming and counseling patients and family members during periods of extreme stress became my specialty. Leaving work at the end of an exhausting day and knowing that I had done my best was very rewarding. A quiet thank-you from a patient's family or from a nurse who appreciated my stepping in to help lift or move a patient was always uplifting.

Still, the hours and the rigorous workload were pushing me close to the edge. I remember saying to myself, "Okay. If you don't get a handle on this thing called 'medicine,' it will destroy you." When I looked at the statistics, I realized that doctors had very high divorce rates and the highest rate of suicide. How could this be? I did not want to get to the point where everything I had worked so tirelessly to obtain became a façade. I needed to have a healthy balance between work and life so that I didn't end up a statistic.

Another personal challenge I experienced was trying to reconcile that I was in the Mecca of health care, the US, with all of its medical advances, yet when my father was sick, he could not get access to any of it. He died earlier than expected because of the limited health-care opportunities in the islands. This really bothered me. There I was, learning about the latest technology and all of the advances in health care, but I couldn't help those closest to me. My own father, in the depths of his illness, did not have access to our superior health-care system.

Eventually, as rewarding as my career was—long shifts, chaos, crisis, and all—I noticed that changes were starting to occur. The workload started increasing, and the powers that be in the hospital started requiring more from doctors. There was also colleague rivalry and no camaraderie within our group, which exacerbated the disparity issues minority doctors faced. We had to be twice as skillful to be considered equal, and at the same time, there was a perception that we were, somehow, afforded the opportunity to practice medicine through affirmative action and, therefore, were not as knowledgeable as nonminority doctors.

It seemed that our challenge was a greater one. Unfortunately, much of this discrimination and disparity came from my colleagues—people who, I thought, should know better. Another challenge was the prevalent disparity in health care. For instance, if patients had means, they were able to get excellent care. If they didn't have means, the care was substandard.

When I first began working at the hospital, I wanted to break this cycle of negativity, especially because of my experience with discrimination in Michigan. I also wanted to break this cycle of negativity in the standard of care for all patients. Despite my best efforts, minority patients and doctors experienced conscious and unconscious discrimination. I felt I had to prove my worth, as if I were always behind the starting line.

After a short time it became clear that some of my colleagues didn't necessarily have my best interests at heart. I'm a dedicated physician, so I would treat my patients and do everything that was required of me when I was in the hospital. But I noticed that others would leave maybe seven patients in the emergency room for me to see. So when I signed out, I would be told, "Oh, and you have seven admissions in the emergency room." I was drowning in work. The focus was no longer on the best patient care but on the number of patients I could see in a given day. I was being worked and worked but did not experience satisfaction from that work. I felt I was doing a disservice to my patients in the hospital.

Another change was occurring among the hospital staff hierarchy, which I started to realize wasn't as equal as I thought it was or should be. There was oversight upon oversight upon oversight. The overseers, though they weren't directly my supervisors, were less qualified. For instance, some physician assistants (PAs) would be in charge of overseeing the physicians, and given my experience and background in the air force, I couldn't understand that chain of command. The rules that had to be followed included a chain of command between supervisors and those of lower rank and status. As I realized this, I began to pay much closer attention to what was going on in the hospital.

This was a challenging time in my career; I had to do a lot of self-talk and self-encouragement. I forced the challenges and difficult things to the back of my mind. I kept them buried so that I could stay focused on my goals. At times, I thought I would never get through that phase in my life, but I am thankful that it forced me to examine why I was doing what I was doing and helped me define my values and purpose.

BEGINNING A PRIVATE PRACTICE

While I struggled through my time at the hospital, I decided to take over a small practice, part-time, on my days off so I could learn more about the business.

I started this small practice after paying a retiring physician $20,000 to take over his patients. I started seeing these patients on the days when I was not working in the hospital. It was just a small practice with one exam room, a little waiting room, and a reception-ist. That's how I learned to see patients in the outpatient setting. I taught myself.

Working in the hospital full-time and working my small practice on the side was not easy to do. My days were long because I spent many hours in the hospital, working twelve-hour shifts. I worked on Saturday, Sunday, Monday, and Tuesday at the hospital and on Wednesday and Thursday at my private practice, where the patient population was small enough to be handled on two or three half-days a week. My experience with my first small practice was a stepping-stone to other practices I would have in the future. I put my best effort into trying to grow my practice and learning about private-practice ownership. Nonetheless, my focus, at the time, was still on my work at the hospital.

My biggest challenges, however, started when the way we practiced medicine began to change. Everyone, from the hospital doctors and staff to the government, started worrying about the cost of health care. It became clear, based on the research, that hospitals were where the majority of health-care dollars went. So with the Affordable Care Act, things started changing.

Hospitals were going to become less profitable as a result of new mandates, so they developed a new business model. They began cutting costs by hiring more PAs instead of physicians, nurse anesthetists instead of anesthesiologists, and so on. Hospitals also invented new revenue streams by cutting off independent community physicians' access to the hospital so they could take over all hospitalized patients, who were now treated by the hospitalist team. Hospitals also started buying up outpatient medical practices, thus forming a legion of employed outpatient physician providers and keeping the revenue in-house. They also began investing in, purchasing, and building urgent-care centers, thus directly competing with independent primary-care providers. Independent primary-care providers were now fighting for survival. How could they practice medicine in the traditional sense, keep the lights on, and still compete with big businesses (i.e., the hospitals)? I understand why so many of my colleagues left private practice to become hospital employees because the prevailing feeling was that if they couldn't beat them, they'd join them.

I felt as if my hands were tied at my level of patient care, and the amount of money we hospitalists, and also the hospital, were making wasn't commensurate with the level of care that we were delivering. This was certainly not the vision of success I had for my career in medicine. I had not worked this hard through medical school, the air force, and residency training to end up practicing medicine this way.

In addition, the hospital now based its standard on volume. Hospital providers now had to see more and more and more patients. There were times when I would begin a shift and end up admitting twenty patients—that is, constant patient admissions. Eventually, the powers that be in the hospital started playing with the salary structure. "You have to see this minimum number of patients," they said, "and only if you see this many patients will you be able to receive a bonus. If you see less, you'll be disincentivized. You'll get less money." This salary structure of shelling out bonuses for the highest number of patients a doctor could see in a day diminished quality of care because doctors were simply exhausted. They suffered burnout.

Then, formulas began appearing, showing the number of patients doctors should see each hour, each shift, and each day, and this was tied to the amount of bonus payment each doctor would receive. Fortunately, for me, by this time, my private practice was growing. I realized that if I could see the patients in my practice and then see them at the hospital if they needed hospitalization, I could sustain myself. This was the need that the patients had, and this arrangement gave great continuity of care. If the patients in my outpatient private practice got sick and were subsequently admitted to the hospital, I, as a community provider, had the option of rounding on my own patients or requesting that the hospital provider (hospitalist) manage my patients while they were in the hospital. Essentially, I could round on my own patients in the hospital and manage their care and, incidentally, have an additional revenue stream. But this system was suddenly disrupted by the new model of hospital-employed providers taking over all patient care.

I viewed myself as a member of the community who was in a position to provide a high standard of care for people who desperately needed it. I also saw this level of patient care as a way to get a better handle on the cost of health care. If you can treat people properly and keep them out of hospitals, you are not only controlling the cost of health care, but patients then get what they need. This is better in the long run for everyone involved. Otherwise, when hospital doctors are assigned too many patients, the results can be rushed, leading to inadequate patient care and lack of proper diagnosis.

Nonetheless, the hospital started challenging my seeing patients in my private practice and then following them to the hospital if they were admitted. The hospital's way of securing the patient population was a monetary thing.

As a primary-care doctor, seeing the patients I saw in the hospital was all of my own accord, and the income was also all mine. This was money I earned because I was the only one doing the work. With my outpatient practice growing at a steady pace at the same time I was working in the hospital and dealing with being overworked by the corporate power structure of the hospital, I began to realize that if I worked smarter, it would be better financially.

The lack of support I received from the hospital made me feel as if I were being pushed out of the hospital. When the administrative staff told me that I could no longer see my patients in the hospital because I was already seeing them in my private practice, I felt as if I were being cut off and pushed out from doing the very thing I always wanted to do: be a physician. I also felt that I was being taken away from patients in the hospital with whom I had already established a relationship. So my first reaction to this ultimatum—that I had to immediately choose between my private practice and the hospital—was an angry one. I took it personally. I asked them why they were pushing me out, and I questioned whether it was because my private practice was successful. Eventually, I had to set those personal feelings of attack aside and realize that it was not about me. Rather, it was a move to push community physicians out of the hospital and change the model to allow only hospital-employed doctors to treat the patients. It was now easy to recognize what they were doing.

Whenever the hospital administration staff members were asked why they were doing this—the same questions I had first asked—they would use different excuses. Ultimately, their goal was to have this new plan of pushing out community physicians implemented within three to five years. Basically, the premise was that older physicians practicing medicine before 1995 were grandfathered into the hospital and could continue to see their patients because they would probably soon retire. If not, they would have to recertify their medical practice through internal-medicine boards and take the necessary exams. After taking these exams, the hospital would require more of them and more and more. The contingencies they were beginning to put in place mostly amounted to ridiculous expectations of physicians who had been practicing medicine for over twenty years. Interestingly enough, physicians across the country revolted against the additional requirements, and the American Board of Internal Medicine suspended the controversial Maintenance of Certification (MOC) requirements through 2018.

Nonetheless, my hospital did not relent. The administrators kept insisting on this new policy, as this was a way of culling the community physicians. They put more pressure on me to make an almost impossible decision: stop rounding at the hospital where I saw the bulk of my patients or take time away from my private practice to pursue even more academic credentials. I chose to continue investing and growing my private practice. I wanted to remain in the trenches and continue taking care of patients. I felt that this was where the need was, and my time was better spent this way rather than memorizing more charts of nebulous information that I would never see in the real world. I still maintained my hospital privileges at several other hospitals; however, my emphasis was now on outpatient medicine.

LAST DAYS IN THE HOSPITAL

Instead of moping and complaining that things were not working out the way I had initially planned, I had to look at the bright side of things: I was now able to pursue the dream I always had of having a full-time, private medical practice. It would just have to happen sooner rather than later. So I made the decision to leave the hospital and devote all of my time and energy to my private practice.

My previous patient population had been broken down into hospitalized patients, nursing-home patients, and office patients. My revenue stream was broken up as follows: 40 percent from hospitalized patients, 30 percent from office patients, and 30 percent from nursing-home or extended-care facility patients.

Consequently, when I stopped working at the hospital and my hospitalized patients were taken from me, I no longer received that income. My income from the hospital was more than 40 percent of my total income, so it was difficult to not feel immediate discouragement and panic. I was trying to survive, build a practice, and raise a young family.

I had to go into self-preservation mode because I could not allow my dream to be hijacked by the hospital in one fell swoop. I had to still ensure that my personal success would be achieved, even beyond a hospital career. Therefore, I had no choice but to try to figure out how to grow my private practice with new patients.

I housed my practice in a leased space. This had already been established before I left the hospital. It helped to have a separate place established so that I didn't have to scramble to find a building. My challenge, however, was to figure out a way to increase my private practice as a sustainable business.

In trying to figure that out, I started using all the tools that I had learned in the air force, and interestingly enough, in track and field as well. I applied the art of command and control I had learned from the military, and from it I learned how to build. I started using an infrastructure model and built my practice from there. In track and field, you have to be strategic when you are preparing for your event, so I also applied those same techniques to my strategy of growing my medical practice.

In my experience, it is very difficult for doctors to agree, so partnerships usually collapse if a robust relationship does not exist. Solo practitioners in private practice are used to complete autonomy and are accustomed to getting paid all earnings after expenses. This expectation does not readily change when practitioners become employees. New owners/investors require some return on their investment and may reduce the level of compensation. This can sometimes leave a bad taste in the mouth of the employed physician. On the other hand, a fixed, guaranteed salary often results in reduced productivity. The solution is command and control with a fair compensation structure and mechanisms in place to reward productivity and penalize low production. From a single command center, we eliminate the infighting and indecisiveness, and we are then able to design a successful operation by identifying the revenue sources, focusing on the customer base and our product/brand, and obtaining financing, thus competing effectively in the market.

I had also recognized from hospital and primary-care practice that *you become a success when you can recognize the strengths and weaknesses in yourself and in your opponent as well.* The hospital was not my enemy or opponent at this point, but I still felt that I had been taken advantage of and given no choice but to leave. As a result, I wanted to devise a plan to grow my private practice without the support of the hospital and also replace the 40 percent of income I had lost. So I started building a business model.

I came up with a one hundred point model on the art of purchasing a practice to build my private practice. I had no choice but to succeed. In fact, I needed to survive. It was do or die because the model for reimbursement by the insurance companies had changed, and everybody was trying to attract patients as a result. You see, population health—an approach to care that aims to improve the health of an entire human population—involves developing individual integrated evaluation and treatment plans for empanelled patients (those for whom a physician or team is responsible). In the United States, the number and mix of primary-care providers must satisfy demand and ensure access to all necessary services. In this new model, the number of patients empanelled determines the amount of the reimbursement from insurance companies, so getting as many patients empanelled in your patient-centered medical home and managing their care is the most cost-effective way to success.

I also realized how important it was for me to establish a new vision for my practice, one that was not what the hospital was doing, one that was wholly focused on patient-centered medical care. It would include the integration of technology, coupled with the building of a robust infrastructure. This was something I knew

I could do, so I began carefully developing my business model for success. Once I had developed my business model, I replicated it in other practices. (I'll give more detailed, step-by-step information about my business model in a later chapter.)

DEVELOPING A MODEL FOR PURCHASING PRACTICES

Calculating the value of a medical practice that is being evaluated for acquisition is controversial at best. The health-care environment continues to evolve, and you now have acquisitions of medical practices, physicians becoming employees, and implementation of the seven wastes of lean—a method that helps identify waste and other types of issues in the workplace. This framework includes defects, transportation, inventory, overprocessing, movement, overproduction, and waiting.

In the 1990s, hospitals developed the integrated delivery network (IDN), which allowed the primary-care provider to be the gatekeeper, the first point of contact. This incentivized the hospitals to purchase medical practices at a high value to ensure referrals without money being paid directly to the doctor, which would have been a direct violation of federal and state antikickback laws. The greatest determinant of the value of a practice at this time was the physician's compensation and expected earning potential. Once they were paid, however, doctors worked less and hospitals lost money. This strategy ultimately failed, and hospitals unloaded medical practices based on the value of the fixed assets (furniture and equipment).

Times have changed since then. Twenty years later, primary-care providers are no longer gate keepers, IDNs are no longer as important, patients can make appointments directly with specialists, specialist-owned outpatient surgical suites now compete directly with hospitals, expenses have increased, and reimbursements have declined. This set the stage for a new round of medical practice acquisitions by hospitals. However, the formula changed. The practice acquisition valuation was based on tangible and intangible assets, and compensation of the now-employed physician was based on a measure of productivity called relative value units (RVUs).

Consequently, I came up with a model of how to evaluate a medical practice for purchase that was different from this. I value the investment that older physicians have put into building their practices and compensate them for that. I look at doctors who are seventy years of age and looking to retire. I look at a specific set of criteria:

- Where are they located?

- Is their practice a part of a gentrification process? (This is the restoration and upgrading of deteriorated urban property by middle-class or affluent people, often resulting in displacement of lower-income people and thus changing the character of the area.)

- Is the practice stable?

- Is it in a deprived area?

I also evaluate the cost of a plan for developing a building as a medical facility. (For example, revamped wiring, new cabinetry, carpeting, refurbished floors, new paint, upgrades to handicapped-accessible areas, expansion of the telecommunications system, etc.)

- What is the competition like (other thriving medical practices)?

- How many patients are they seeing?

- Which insurance providers are they accepting: Medicare, Medicaid, Blue Cross Blue Shield, United Health Care, and so on?

This is my basis for determining if a practice is worth evaluating for a possible purchase or take-over. Can I build and stretch my business model for private practice from it? Each of these are important factors for me to consider.

I dedicated ten years to my hospital career before I left it (2001–2011). When my hospital career ended, I felt I was just as smart as those hospital CEOs, if not smarter, and I could do better working for myself and being the CEO of my own practice. Yes, it was a better opportunity for me to be my own CEO. After all, this is the heart of true entrepreneurship. But I had a lot to learn. When I created a new model of private medical-practice success, I thought that all I needed to do was replicate and transfer the model the hospital had set up. I soon realized that the hospital's business model was not the wave of the future, and I would need to create and develop a new kind of business model for private practice that merged business with traditional patient care.

Eventually, I reevaluated my model and came up with an idea of what a medical practice would be worth, and I started putting that idea into place. I'd approach doctors with struggling practices and offer to help them upgrade their technology and electronic medical records (EMRs) with practice management and by training their staff. I would also offer them the opportunity to sell or to be employed by my organization. By consolidating and revamping the infrastructure, investing in technology, developing and training a robust staff, making wise business decisions, and weathering tough times, I was able to create a patient-centered medical home. Armed with a strong track record and a profitable beta site, I was now ready for expansion.

When evaluating a medical practice, there are many variables to consider, which makes it difficult to compare one practice to another. Also, evaluation methods are highly dependent on what is important to the physician purchasing the practice. One doctor may focus more on revenue generation, another on location or reputation. It is important to do the research and to ask the right questions initially, which should include but are not limited to:

- What is the annual revenue?

- What fees are collected?

- What is the practice overhead?

- Is there room for streamlining?

- How is the practice structured?

- Are there deteriorating revenues in the most recent year?

- Is the practice stable? (See the previous section subheaded "Developing a Model for Purchasing Practices")

After these initial questions, a lot of it depends on "kicking the tires" and "gut instinct" (i.e., if the hairs on the back of my neck stand up, and I genuinely feel in my heart and soul that something is wrong, then it usually is). Even with lots of research, you will never know exactly what you're going to get. You can only do your best to minimize the risk.

Approaches for calculating the value/purchase price of a medical practice include:

1. **Income approach:** estimated cash flow

2. **Market approach:** a review of competing practices

3. **Cost approach:** the cost of recreating the practice, also known as the start-up practice value

I used a combination of several approaches to come up with a reliable practice-evaluation model.

I came up with what a medical practice should be worth by comparing existing formulas, realizing what was being excluded or inappropriately added, and devising my own "Richardson formula." Existing formulas include the following:

---

1. **Value equals between 1 and 1.25 times the annual gross revenue.**

2. **Value equals adjusted net cash flow times the amortization factor** (a statistical summation of the terms and conditions of a credit accommodation, principle ratio, and term of a loan).

3. **Value equals average annual gross revenues times .65** (standard medical/dental advance rate of projections).

4. **Value equals intangible assets plus tangible assets plus physician compensation.**

    Tangible assets include equipment (whether new or outdated), **furniture, cash, prepaid insurances/ unexpired insurance premiums, and revenue**

minus expenses (payroll taxes, loans, retirement plan contributions, accounts receivable, office building). If the office building is leased, the value is dependent on the number of years remaining, the amount paid for rent compared to the current market rate, and the ability to renew. **Intangible assets include referral patterns/referral network, the seller staying with the practice, goodwill, insurance mix or payer profile, economic climate, fair-market value compensation for physician or his/her replacement, office location, parking, profitability, active patient population, patient charts, medical group management, provider productivity, Centers for Medicare and Medicaid Services (CMS) fee schedule, and distribution of providers in catchment area.**

The Richardson formula encompasses all the above with data added for a more accurate and current practice evaluation.

Not many, if any, of these medical practices used modern technology in terms of EMRs. I, therefore, implemented a technology infrastructure into the practice by utilizing patient electronic records that could be accessed by the doctor with one click on the computer. By bringing the practice up to speed and by reaching out to the existing patient population, I was—and still am—able to create a sustainable practice. Technology integration is my competitive advantage. Embracing technology allows me to effectively reach out to the retained patient population and also allows effective time and data management. These guys were sitting on little gold mines and they didn't even know it. They just needed to be taught how to access the treasure. Thankfully, I knew how.

Acquiring practices allowed me to build my patient population. Moreover, the technology allowed me to effectively manage a larger-than-average patient panel by having all of the patient data readily available. This allowed me to build my patient population return so that I was able to see the same number of patients I previously had. And then, once I realized that it worked, I was motivated to try it again and keep trying it. That was how the practices expanded into even more than I could have imagined.

RESISTANCE TO CHANGE

Acquiring these practices did not mean, though, that I did not face pushback from other physicians after I left the hospital. One of the things I did as my practice grew was share space with a group of physicians. These physicians, however, did not agree with my business structure. They did not want to rock the boat by introducing technology and EMRs to the practice. I had already gotten to the point where I recognized that medicine was changing and we needed to integrate technology.

They completely disagreed with me, so I tried to demonstrate the value of these innovations. I implemented the technology, and I showed them how we could be more profitable if we were more economical with our time and also what we could do with our practices for the future. In fact, at this present time, a key provision of the American Recovery and Reinvestment Act of 2009 is in effect. All public and private health-care providers and other eligible professionals must have adopted and demonstrated "meaningful use" of EMRs, as defined by HealthIT.gov. Digital medical and health records must be used to improve quality, safety, and efficiency, and reduce health disparities; engage patients and family; improve care coordination, population, and public health; and maintain privacy and security of patient-health information. Penalties exist for noncompliance. Eligible professionals who haven't implemented Electronic Medical Records (EMR), Electronic Health Records (EHR), and Personal Health Records (PHR) systems and demonstrated their meaningful use by 2015 will experience a 1 percent reduction in Medicare reimbursements, and rates of reduction will rise annually thereafter.

An EMR is a digital version of the paper chart and is more beneficial than paper records because it allows providers to track data over time, identify patients who are due for preventable visits and screenings, and monitor how patients measure up to certain parameters and improved accessibility and organization of data. An EHR is built to go beyond standard clinical data and is inclusive of a broader view of a patient's care. A PHR includes the same information as the EHR but is set up, accessed, and managed by patients.

Nonetheless, my colleagues still rejected these impending changes. Not only did I get pushed out of my primary hospital, but I was also being pushed aside by people who I thought were my colleagues and comrades in the field of medicine. The climate was hostile, and I felt as if I were a lone ranger. The majority of my colleagues believed EMRs were a waste of time. Apprehensive, dismissive, and afraid, they questioned investing additional money in technology that was changing every day when profit margins were already slim. I knew this resistance was happening when I tried to implement new systems, but I had to look at the long-term benefits of investing additional money in building the technological side of the medical practice.

My colleagues were especially upset when I said, "Let's come up with a succession plan in which I can take over your practices, and you'll get a golden parachute (an employment contract specification promising large benefits to the employee in the event that the company is acquired and the employment is terminated). Such a benefit can take the form of severance pay, a bonus, stock options, or a combination thereof. I told my colleagues that I would ensure the same net annual income. They didn't really expect that this young upstart would dare say that to them or could even accomplish it. My meeting with them ended badly. It got ugly, arguments ensued, and we eventually had to part ways. These people were the naysayers who could very well deter my hopes.

I wasn't happy, of course, that my approach turned out the way it did. These were professionals whom I respected and wanted to work with. However, everything happens for a reason, and I couldn't allow disagreements to deter my success and the goals I had in mind for my medical practice. I also came to understand that at this time, other physicians just couldn't fathom changing the traditional medical structure to which they had grown so accustomed. They feared implementing the technology. When I thought more about it, I realized they weren't necessarily angry with me, nor did they think I was changing the face of medicine. Rather, they were most likely just afraid of stepping forward and using a new type of model for medicine. They feared what was coming and, in turn, feared to embrace it. But therein lay the business opportunity. And I seized it.

This negative experience fueled my ambitions and allowed me to branch out completely on my own and start building medical practices by going back to the traditional art of medicine: maintaining a small, intimate setting while also implementing, in the background, an infrastructure that supported everything. This meant that the infrastructure and technology within the medical practice would support the entire operation. I thought, *I'm right here; I know exactly how to do this. All I need is financing.* I had already started doing this on my own, beyond my first private practice, so I had the confidence to get it done and see it through. I had done it on my own, on a small scale, and it was working. But for this model to be scalable, to get to the next level where I could have, say, fifty medical practices in twenty-four months, I needed help. I needed to be able to pay for the infrastructure that I needed.

This was the next level I needed to reach. And I had to do it well without losing sight of my original goal of maintaining traditional medical practices, focusing on the best patient care in a small, intimate setting, and merging those practices with a thriving business model. This was the point at which I did a lot of soul searching into my past and envisioning how that past would shape my future and how I saw the future of medicine.

PEARL #4:
Find your purpose.

PART 2

A PARADIGM SHIFT

CHAPTER 5

RETURNING TO THE TRADITIONAL

What counts in life is not the mere fact that we have lived.
It is what difference we have made to the lives of others
that will determine the significance of the life we led.
—Nelson Mandela

D uring my residency, throughout my training and into my hospital career, I worked on tracing my family's ancestry. At first, it was a project I wanted to complete but was not eager to begin. However, after I left hospital work, I was determined to learn even more about the maternal and paternal side of my family and trace the significance of my roots. From whom had I descended? Where did I come from? What were the importance of those traits and characteristics in me? I needed to find out exactly who I was—the part the public doesn't see and the part I sometimes struggle with and question. There is significance, a great lasting value, in understanding your past. I believe it enables you to confidently enter your future with a plan of success.

And so began a new journey for me.

TRACING MY ANCESTRY

When I began, I used historical records and oral histories. I later added DNA studies and traced the Y chromosomes in my male relatives and the mitochondria in my female ancestors. This method produced some distinct lineages, mainly my direct paternal ancestry but also my maternal ancestry. I actually traced a few different branches of my family tree. I traced my father's father, my father's mother, my mother's father, and my mother's mother. In doing this, I found that my family tree embodied the West Indian culture, which is a mixture of cultures. I now know that my paternal grandmother's ancestry was Irish because of DNA evidence as well as the fact that Anguilla is made up of descendants from Ireland, Africa, and the native Carib people. I also know that my maternal grandmother's ancestors came from a region of Sierra Leone in Africa and were Mende, as in the Mende Tribe.

Traditional Bamileke tunic.
Photographer: Leonard
Richardson M.D.

The bulk of my research came from my father's side. This was where I found the most fascinating and detailed account of my roots and, consequently, my purpose. My father's side of the family showed a direct link to Bamileke Cameroon and Egypt. On his side were the Bamileke people. I did not know much, if anything, about this group of people, but naturally, I wanted to learn more. I researched who these people were, and I found out that they were very enterprising people with a very strong entrepreneurial spirit who lived in West Cameroon. About two-thirds of them spoke French, the Franco-Bamileke, and the remaining one-third spoke English, the Anglo-Bamileke.

I started inquiring, meeting, and wondering more about my African ancestry. I began to ask more and more questions. I acquired a wealth of information about my Egyptian ancestry, dating back thousands of years. My father's people left Egypt in the ninth century and moved down the Nile River. It turns out that with the spread of Islam into Egypt, this group had to choose whether to convert to Islam or leave. They chose to leave and travel south through Sudan and settle in Northern Cameroon. Under pressure from the Fulani invasions in the seventeenth century, they were forced to move further south and to the west, where they settled in West Cameroon, in the grasslands. That's how they ended up in West Cameroon, and they have lived there since the seventeenth century.

This opened the door to my finding even more about who these people in Egypt were. That's when I started looking at DNA haplotypes of the Y chromosome and found that the same genetic haplotype had recently been discovered in mummies from the thirteenth dynasty, the dynasty of Ramses III. I came to realize that there was a direct link with my DNA and the mummies in Egypt, which was fascinating to me. When you look at natural history, and you go back to the days of the cavemen, you see that men, initially, learned to communicate by hunting together and, essentially, surviving together. They

Statue of Imhotep.
Source: egyptianmythology.org

learned to draw on cave walls to further communicate. Fast forward thousands of years to the first great civilization in the chain of great civilizations is that of the Egyptians, who developed the papyrus and hieroglyphics. By studying this history and the societal progression of my ancestors beyond just tracing my Y chromosome, I learned of Ramses III and of Imhotep, a well-known figure in ancient Egyptian medicine described as the "author of a medical treatise remarkable for being devoid of magical thinking" (*Wikipedia*). Hippocrates is most widely known and referred to as the father of medicine, but Imhotep was also the father of medicine.

From Cameroon, at about the same time as the Fulani invasion, a male ancestor of mine was taken from his people, sold into slavery, and crossed the Atlantic ocean during the transatlantic slave trade. He subsequently landed in the Caribbean, which led to my Caribbean history in St. Kitts and Anguilla. This knowledge of Egypt, Cameroon (African influences), and the Caribbean (British, Irish, and French influ-

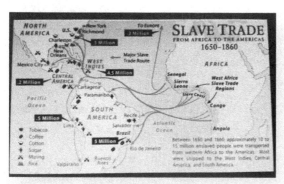

Slave trade from Africa to the Americas.
Source: Dr. Neil A Frankel's The Atlantic Slave Trade & Slavery in America; maps of Africa

ences) produced in me a strong sense of self-determination. It also gave me a strong sense of purpose.

I've now gone back to 3000 BC, tracing my ancestry from Cameroon to Egypt, to the origins of medicine when the first known doctor was documented. The Greeks and the Romans are famous for helping to develop mathematics. The Romans developed modern writing tools and names for planets and months of the calendar.

However, this new knowledge that I had gained about my African and Egyptian heritage revealed that my people also contributed much to mankind's advancement. This, of course, made me very proud. I found out that I had a direct linkage to the early part of medicine, the earliest medical scholars, which I found absolutely fascinating.

The more I found out about my ancestry, the more certain I became that what I was doing as a physician was what I was called to do—and anything less would mean not achieving my full potential. With this renewed purpose, I realized that, essentially, I had "made it." I had accomplished my dreams as the result of the genetic drive within me. And moving forward, I wanted to create something that would be profitable and long lasting for generations after me, including my children.

I hadn't entered the field of medicine only because I wanted to make my father proud or to achieve something that appeared to the world as a great accomplishment. I probably would not have put forth the rigorous effort I did in the air force, medical school, or residency training if these had been my reasons. Without a shadow of a doubt, I knew that the path I had taken up to that point was all a part of my destiny. It was what I was destined to do.

LINKED TO MY PURPOSE

Spending ten years learning about my ancestry and essentially growing up and maturing through the entire process birthed in me a new vision for the type of person and physician I wanted to be. I truly loved what this ten-year journey of tracing my family roots had done *to* me and *for* me. With my passion and vision for medicine now renewed, I looked at my profession through a new lens. I was no longer just somebody going in, seeing patients, and then going home.

I now wanted to know the *why*, the nuts and bolts of how things functioned and how I could be a part of the solution to make the field of medicine and patient care much better. I wanted to know what was going on in Annapolis, the home of Maryland's legislature, where I lived. What was going on with the medical care of our military? What was going on in Congress? What was truly going on in medicine? I needed to understand all of this if I wanted to be ahead of the curve.

I needed to take the enthusiasm and energy that I had—my renewed passion for medicine—and develop my brand. I was going to be an entrepreneur and develop medicine as I thought it should be developed because I was viewing it through the lens of my experiences. I also recognized that medical practices lacked the current business model. These traditional medical practices were the sum total of my medical knowledge, skills, and practice. They were based on the theories, beliefs, and experiences indigenous to the individual cultures of my diverse patient population and used in the maintenance of their health as well as in the prevention, diagnosis, improvement, and treatment of physical and mental illness.

Looking deeply into these facets of my life and the business model I was trying to develop, I was also forced to reevaluate how I viewed traditional medicine and how it would affect my medical practice. In order for you to understand how my view of traditional medicine changed, I should first define traditional medicine for you. The definition of *traditional medicine* by the World Health Organization is as follows: "Traditional medicine is the sum total of the knowledge, skills, and practices based on the theories, beliefs, and experiences indigenous to different cultures, whether explicable or not, used in the maintenance of health, as well as in the prevention, diagnosis, improvement, or treatment of physical and mental illness."

My interpretation of traditional medicine was that it was *culturally sensitive, intimate, and patient centered.* My intention was to continue to focus on everything that encompassed this original definition of traditional medicine. I would be practicing preventive medicine—diagnosing and treating both physical and mental illness and also the spiritual life of my patients. My practice would also still involve complete, thorough training in the skills of Western medicine and aligning with best practices, industry standards, and evidence-based medicine. I would still be doing all of this but with an emphasis on making the patient feel whole, creating intimate, small settings, and taking away the chaos of what had now become commercial medicine led by large hospitals.

Shang gong zhi wei bing, zhong gong zhi yi bing zhe. This means that the superior doctor treats when there is no disease, and the mediocre doctor treats when disease appears. Practitioners of Chinese medicine believe that physicians should not treat via palliative care but should, instead, seek the root cause and mechanism of the disease. I encompass this in my brand by including cultural, social, and economic factors in the delivery of care. I emphasize the importance of community, traditions, focus, and meaning in one's life. I teach healthy dietary habits, exercise techniques, and resilience. The goal is to shift the mind-set from illness to health and well-being.

So, you may ask, did my view of traditional medicine change after researching my past? I would say that it became more holistic. The holistic view of medicine considers the whole person and the quest for optimal health and wellness. We should strive for balance in mind, body, spirit, and emotions. If one of these is out of balance, then the overall health of the patient is adversely affected. My quest for self-discovery allowed me to fully understand that all individuals have innate healing powers and that the whole person should be treated—not just the disease or the disease process. It also helped me to focus on the cause of the imbalance/illness and not just on symptom relief. Healing involves the provider and the patient working as a team.

The value of the doctor-patient relationship in terms of *honesty, a sense of belonging (happiness), and consistency* are the top three values of the doctor-patient relationship. They are the bedrock of traditional medicine. Honesty is important to one's health because we need to be honest with ourselves and with one another in order to know where we stand.

Happiness is very important, and we should be honest with ourselves as we strive for this. Happiness is different from pleasure, and we should know the difference. A warm bath can be pleasurable, but who wants to stay in a bathtub for twenty-four hours? At some point it becomes unpleasant. Not so with happiness. Henry David Thoreau said, "Happiness is like a butterfly. The more you chase it, the more it will elude you, but if you turn your attention to other things, it will come and sit softly on your shoulder." My feeling, however, is that happiness can be pursued.

We can all increase our "set point" (i.e., pursuing happiness) by rejecting pessimism, resentment, and anger and instead embracing optimism, gratitude, and compassion. This is how we secure happiness, emotional freedom, and resilience. Consistency in diet, exercise, psychotherapy, relationships, spiritual counseling, and managing stress are also important and will lead to improved overall health.

I also understand that medicine will continue to evolve. What we know today as best practice will not be what we do in ten years and twenty years from now. The objective is to continue to study and research to find the best medicines and interventions to treat illnesses while, at the same time, trying to make our patients feel whole and improve their conditions.

Allowing people to have access to health care was paramount in order to meet this objective. So I started coming up with models of how we could improve the care of the 5 percent of patients who are not getting the health care they need but are costing 50 percent of the health-care dollars in the United States. According to the Centers for Medicare and Medicaid Services, these are the things that are driving health-care costs out of control. Let me explain further. As policy makers consider various ways to contain the rising cost of health care, it is useful to examine the patterns of spending on health care throughout the United States. In 2004, the United States spent $1.9 trillion, or 16 percent of its gross domestic product (GDP), on health care. This averages out to about $6,280 for each man, woman, and child. However, actual spending is distributed unevenly across individuals, different segments of the population, specific diseases, and payers. This is an increase from $1,106 per person in 1980 ($255 billion overall and 9 percent of the GDP). During this period, health-care costs grew faster than the economy as a whole. Half of the population spends little or nothing on health care, while 5 percent of the population (civilian, noninstitutionalized) spends almost half of the total amount (49 percent). (See the US Department of Health and Human Services Agency for Health Care Research and Quality chart below.)

CHART SHOWING ANALYSIS OF HEALTH-CARE SPENDING PATTERNS

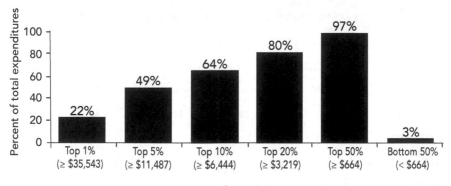

Source: Center for Financing, Access, and Cost Trends, AHRQ

Analysis of health-care spending patterns sheds important light on how best to focus efforts to help restrain rising health-care costs. Recognition that a relatively small group of individuals account for a large fraction of spending in Medicare, Medicaid, private plans, and the population as a whole serves to inform more focused cost-containment strategies. Research also continues to raise awareness of the importance of chronic conditions in overall spending and, as a major driver of cost increases, leads to disease-management programs and other efforts to improve quality and reduce the costs of conditions such as diabetes, asthma, hypertension, heart disease, and obesity.

The current model of hospital-owned practices and urgent-care-center proliferation does not address this disparity. The chickens have come home to roost: decades of health-care disparity helped to produce this problem. One solution may be to incentivize the independent primary-care providers who are already in these hard-to-reach communities to provide primary care instead of allowing large institutions to put them out of business. Small independent practices cannot compete against billion-dollar organizations.

Moreover, I started researching and thinking about ways in which we could improve the health-care system in the Caribbean as well in order to give the islands access to the best care in the world. One of these ways for improvement is telemedicine, telecommunication, and information technologies providing clinical health care at a distance—and integrative medicine and technology. This technology would aid in eliminating distance barriers and improve access to medical services that are often not consistently available in remote rural or hard-to-reach communities. It could also be used to save lives in critical and emergency situations. I started bringing in what I learned in the air force and came up with proposals to do aerospace medicine and transfer patients to a tertiary-level center. (My vision, however, was bigger than my pocket.)

My business model also came from watching the air force handle millions of soldiers. I questioned how we take care of our soldiers around the world. What is the medical system that we use? We can transport a patient, or we can treat in place. Somebody who is injured in Balad or Fallujah can be urgently evacuated, and that soldier can, in turn, be given the best care at Walter Reed or Bethesda. At these primary-level, secondary-level, and tertiary-level facilities, we use state-of-the-art transportation and critical care air transport (CCATT) teams. Through the use of telemedicine, a physician can be in Washington, DC, while also helping to care for a patient in a war zone.

Why not then transfer some of this technology to the civilian world, to areas that are remote, such as the Caribbean, where you don't have access to the same level of medical care? I soon understood that all it took was just the vision and the know-how. This was an opportunity for me to pen my business model idea and present it to the people.

The doctor-patient relationship is defined as primary-care providers taking care of the community and the family. They serve as the social worker, the priest, the community father figure, and so on. The most important word to heed in the phrase *doctor-patient relationship* is the word *relationship*. It is a relationship built on trust in which you have to be consistent with the patients. You have to be honest with them so that they can trust you. And if they trust you, and if you are honest, then they will be very loyal, and that's where that sense of belonging comes in. Your practice then becomes a place to which they go not only be treated physically but also to be treated emotionally. And that is the "sense of belonging" that I'm talking about. So, ideally, in a medical practice, what you're trying to create is a sort of oasis where the patients feel they belong. You're not trying to create a sterile environment. The difficulty lies in doing that for a large group of patients. The model I've developed is the answer.

My office practice model includes establishing a back office that utilizes modern technology. Ideally, by developing this back office, all of the administrative functions will be maintained. What this does is create the ambience of an intimate patient setting in the front medical suite where the physician can focus on the patients, and the patients are not bothered by anything else around them. A symbiotic relationship develops between the physician and those patients. They're on a first-name basis, and they trust each other, and that's when the best care happens. You see, in medical practice, the physician is vested in the patient. Conversely, in the hospital model, the physician is transient. Moreover, in the emergency room, the patients are also transient along with transient physicians. As a result, there is no relationship, and when there is no relationship, patients and physicians are not comfortable.

Consistency is difficult to achieve using the corporate structure of traditional medicine. Hospital physicians work on a shift basis. I did this for ten years, so I understand it. If I'm on duty from seven in the morning to seven in the evening, at the end of my shift, I sign out to another doctor who's coming in. So let's say family members come in and they want to find out what's going on with the patient—this new doctor has to now go and look at my notes, reassess the patient, talk with the patient, and try to figure out what's going on. This can be a problem because if my notes aren't extremely thorough or if there's a misinterpretation of what's going on or miscommunication, then errors in the administration of care can occur during this handoff.

Continuity helps you know your patients. When the hospital calls me and says, "We have patient Jones here. What's going on?" I can say, "Oh, Miss Jones just needs so-and-so." And I can pull information from the recesses of my mind or from my notes because I have continuity of care with my patients. I can inform staff of anything that may be different for this patient.

But the way medicine is now practiced takes community physicians away from the hospitalized or extended-care facility patient encounter. Patients have become more isolated. The institutional memory of primary-care physicians and the trust they built with their patients is severed. Continuity and consistency is diminished, causing disjointed care. I believe that this hinders the ability to provide patients with the best care. The goal of my business model is to bring health care back to that continuity of care.

TRADITIONAL MEDICINE WITHIN A SUCCESSFUL BUSINESS MODEL

So can traditional medicine and technology merge with business to create a successful business model and the best continuity of care? Is this possible? The answer is yes! Yes, it can happen with a robust support structure. Most physicians in a hospital and in private practice are compassionate and would love to give their patients the best care. The challenge is handling all the minutia, government regulations, paperwork, call backs, scheduling, and phones. All those administrative tasks that must be addressed can take away from the doctor-patient encounter. My opportunity is to provide robust practice-management support that frees physicians to do what they do best: being intimately involved with their patients and focusing on patient care. When implemented the right way, my model is seamless. It integrates but is nonintrusive. It takes into account so many aspects of medicine and the real, complicated, unique world that is medical management.

The truth is the traditional way of practicing medicine doesn't work profitably by itself because providers are not reimbursed by third-party payers for time spent doing a thorough, holistic patient evaluation. Traditional practice lacks balance. I've had to figure out what that balance is. What's the size of the infrastructure you need to practice good medicine and keep the lights on?

I've developed a formula for that.

Physicians are a very unique breed. Most of us think we know everything. Some of us don't know that we don't know, and we don't know how to ask for help if we don't know that we need it. As a result, some of us end up just working in or for a hospital. We either become totally employed, or we become independent and try to micromanage everything. This can turn into a problem because we now have to deal with billing, scheduling, inventory, housekeeping, and human resources while, at the same time, providing great patient care.

The middle ground is what is missing. This is where there is an opportunity. How can you still practice medicine in the outpatient setting? How can you escape the inpatient setting when it's run by a corporate structure that's a two billion-dollar hospital, and now you're employed with no autonomy? How can you maintain autonomy, be honest, and have great patient relationships while, at the same time, being successful?

My military experience has helped me to create and organize this entire model of business success for physicians in private practice. The military really helped to teach me command structure where orders/plans are transmitted down the chain of command until they are received by those expected to execute the orders. First, I looked at the resources that needed managing. Then I looked at the manpower, the funds, and the equipment.

THE ART OF LEADERSHIP/EXECUTIVE MANAGEMENT

- display exemplary conduct
- communicate processes
- train, develop, and discipline team members
- enforce standards
- maintain a healthy climate
- manage resources:
    - manpower
    - funds
    - equipment
    - facilities
    - supplies
    - employee time
- align strategically
- generate processes
- inspect programs
- make data-driven decisions
- Avoid:
    - lack of accountability
    - favoritism
    - lack of communication
    - micro managing

"A lot of things can be done with kindness, at least the first two times"   —Col. Camp

I looked at business factors such as knowing your employees so that they are optimally placed. These are all things that you learn in the command structure. You also learn such things as:

- strategic alignment

- process generation

- system assessment

- command inspector program

- decisions about data or practice-management software

I also understood that I had to have a mission statement; I had to have a vision. I needed to know what my goals would be as well as construct a constraint analysis and a SWOT analysis, which is an approach to solving business problems that identifies strengths, weaknesses, opportunities, and threats facing a company; while strengths and weaknesses are internal factors, opportunities and threats are external. Then I needed my metrics. All of this was preparation for the opportunities and targets that I had to have laid out. I wanted to offer physicians the option that once they put my business model in place for their practice, they would have all of these factors at work to help support the practice. But first, I needed to ensure that my model would actually work.

IMPROVING PROCESS PLAN

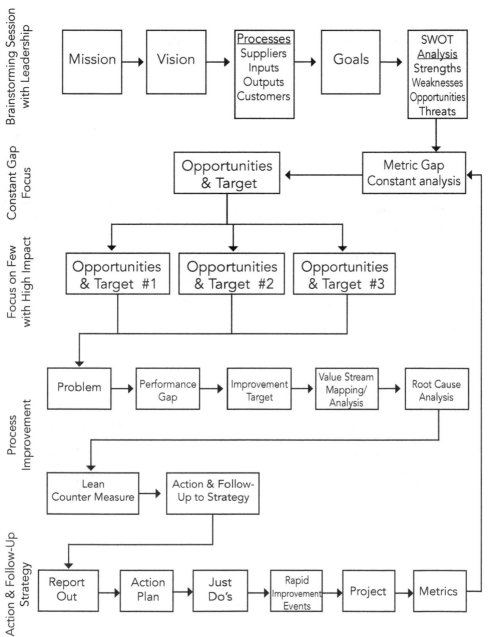

"If you know the enemy and know yourself, your need not fear the results of a hundred battles."

—SunTsu

SCALING UP

My business model had to work for multiple medical practices. First, I tweaked my business plan to the outpatient setting, and it seemed to work. It worked on a small scale, so I did it again and noticed that it was scalable. That's how I moved from one small practice to, now, six successful practices consolidated to form a patient-centered medical home. When I put everything in place, worked out the kinks, and achieved a proven track record that my business model was scalable, I knew it was time to take it to the global level.

My model had to be something that other entrepreneurs could utilize. I had complete confidence that it would work because I had lived it and seen it work. In fact, I knew that my business model could change the world of health care.

My only hesitancy, initially, came when the question of money was considered. For this model to be continuously effective, there has to be financing. It works perfectly on a small scale; I can continue to follow it for the rest of my life and be successful on this scale. However, to not just be successful but also really make a difference, to reach that 5 percent of the US population that is not receiving proper health care, to revamp the health-care system in the Caribbean, I must have buy-ins. My business model needs investment.

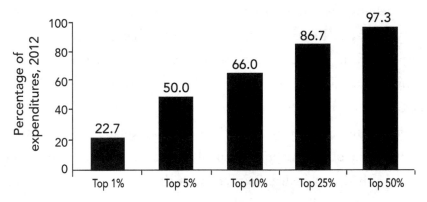

CONCENTRATION OF HEALTH-CARE EXPENDITURES US POPULATION, 2012

Source: Center for Financing, Access and Cost Trends, AHRQ, Household Component of the Medical Expenditure Panel survey (HC-155), 2012

The figure above shows that 1 percent of the population is responsible for 22.7 percent of health-care expenditures, and 5 percent is responsible for 50 percent of all health-care expenditures.

Let's talk more about that 5 percent: 5 percent of the population of the United States does not have access to proper preventative care. Currently, when you look at the astronomical cost of health care, you realize that this 5 percent of patients accounts for 50 percent of the health-care costs. Work is being carried out to create a model to reach this 5 percent and reduce the cost of health care. The traditional model is a fee-for-service in which you treat patients who have this financial access.

The entities that are addressing this problem are corporations, and the government has provided grants. Corporations are looking at the problem as a purely opportunistic way to make money. Unfortunately, they are not in the trenches; they're not the ones who can reach out to these people. Rather, it's the small primary-care doctors who are in these communities, who are not getting reimbursed. They are the people who are attending patients in their own communities and helping meet their needs. My model offers a way to empower these doctors. The traditional model must change from reimbursing specialists with astronomical amounts of money while giving primary-care doctors inadequate compensation to giving primary-care doctors the tools that they need to provide the best care for their patients while at the same time being adequately compensated. Perhaps, the only way the traditional medical authorities will see the problem is if they realize that reform is the key to reducing health-care spending and increasing the quality of patient care.

PROVIDER MODEL FOR ALLOCATION OF RESOURCES

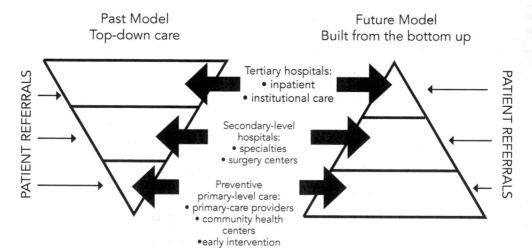

My model is a revolutionary model because it is applicable to more than just one hospital taking care of a group of patients in one community. I can now put a physician, or PA, or nurse practitioner in an area that's underserved, and I can provide the infrastructure to support the vision of my business model joined with traditional medical practices. My system treats patients outside the prestigious medical institutions, which can sometimes be intimidating and complicated for patients to navigate.

Small providers need resources and help. My new model provides support to physicians and physician extenders. For instance, in the state of Maryland, nurse practitioners can now practice solo and independently. But why aren't they doing it? Nobody understands the infrastructure and what it takes to do it. So this is where the opportunity is: my company, Kingdom Medicine, PA, through the use of my business model, is able to build the necessary infrastructure while building a doctor's medical practice to reach the masses.

While discovering more about my ancestry, I was able to discover so much more about myself.

I had to go backward to move forward. I set out to change the model of business and private practice, and in doing so, a renewed passion for patient care developed within me and catapulted my desire to create a sustainable business model implemented within working private practices.

PEARL #5:
Learn from failure.

Chapter 6

HOW I DEVELOPED MY BUSINESS MODEL

If you give me a fish, you feed me for a day. If you teach me to fish you have fed me until the river is contaminated or the shoreline seized for development, but if you teach me to organize, then whatever the challenge is, I can join together with my peers, and we will fashion our own solution.
—adapted from a Chinese proverb,
in *The Barefoot Guide to Working with Organisations and Social Change, vol.* 1

When I researched and fully understood my Egyptian ancestry and the entrepreneurial spirit of the Bamileke people, I gained the inspiration that I needed to continue on my success journey. In addition, I was very enthusiastic about thoroughly looking at what a successful business model would look like. I created a three-part business model of medical management for my private practice. This business model would resemble a Venn diagram with its three separate yet related parts. I've coined it my *logic diagram*. It shows all possible logical relations between the different sets of a finite collection. The first circle reflects one's legacy (history, spirit); the second circle reflects the landscape (legislature, language); and the third circle reflects entrepreneurship (mathematics, energy).

LOGIC DIAGRAM

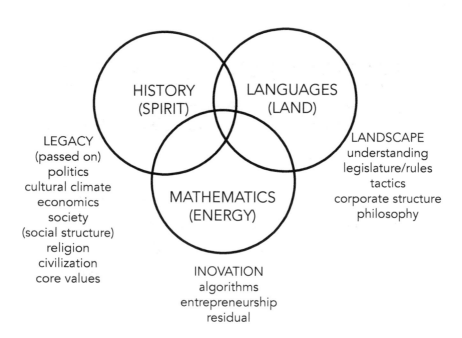

The first part of my business model is understanding your *legacy*, your past. I understood my legacy and was ready to launch into the next phase of life that would bring success. The next step that I focused on was having a complete understanding of my *landscape*, my environment. This is the second part of my business model. The third part is *energy*. This is, essentially, the implementation part.

THE HISTORY BEHIND THE LOGIC DIAGRAM BUSINESS MODEL

So where did I get this idea of my Venn diagram business model? Well, the history behind the model is one of the reasons I wanted to dig deep into my ancestry. I was trying to understand how to move forward and how to survive in the current medical environment. From my data searches and from reading many books over the years, one book really grabbed my attention: *China's Management Revolution* by Charles-Edouard Bouée. In his book, Bouée talks about *spirit, land, and energy* as the basis for success. Immediately, I was drawn to the concepts discussed in the book, and I delved into it, focusing on one idea at a time. This book was my inspiration, and from it, I developed the idea of a business model made up of three components. Each component would represent the three success ideas that Bouée addressed in his book.

PART 1: LEGACY

The first component, previously mentioned, is an understanding of your spirit, or your legacy. Understanding your legacy means having a deep level of understanding of your past and the heroes who have gone before you.

When I was looking into my legacy, I had a unique lens through which to look at things. Growing up in the Caribbean, we have a very proud and very integrative culture that involves many different cultures/ethnicities from around the world; it is in our DNA. Our culture evolved from our African, Indian, European, and Chinese ancestry. I am who I am because of these cultures.

When I talk about the patient-centered medical practice, a part of that is cultural. For me, this is twofold because I have a Caribbean side and also an American side. Now, being American and being considered African American is also unique because this community of people has been disadvantaged for centuries and yet has been able to face adversity and come through successfully.

Armed with this legacy, I now had the core value, the first part of the logic diagram, developed. This would be my foundation for my business model. I understood the politics, the cultural elements, the religion, and the shared core values. So, armed with that information and its multidimensional nature, I was ready to continue developing my model by tackling the second leg, the landscape.

PART 2: LANDSCAPE

Once I understood the first circle of the Venn diagram, the second component was understanding the landscape, which included knowing my environment and the rules of the land. This meant I would need full knowledge of my local legislature. Understanding the landscape is the ability to understand where you are and how to speak the language. I had to learn the corporate structure, the philosophy of where I was, and the philosophy of the patients and the caregivers. This is where my military training came into play because I now understood that communication was key. Of communication, George Bernard Shaw once said, "The single biggest problem with communication is the illusion that it has taken place." *Effective* communication is hugely important.

When you communicate effectively, you are speaking the language of power. Speaking this language means that you must understand where you are, and you have to be able to speak fluently so that other people—your colleagues, your customers, those in the power structure and the infrastructure—understand exactly what's going on. That means you have to understand the rules of engagement and the philosophy of those with whom you're dealing.

You must also understand the culture. Something as simple as handing change back to people by putting it in their hand versus putting it on the counter could mean something totally different in different cultures. Waving your left hand at somebody means hello in the United States, but it is an insult in some Middle Eastern countries. Body language and the cadence and rhythm of one's speech and tone can all be misinterpreted. It is our responsibility to make sure that we understand the art of communication, the art of language, and the landscape of where we are.

This is where I think being in the military helped because military personnel have to deal with people from many different cultures, and one of the things that I was trained to do was to avoid insulting people. I learned to speak the language. I may not be fluent, but at least I learned not to insult people. The second tenet that I learned from my military experience was how to build the infrastructure for my company. I learned the corporate language, which is the art of command. I also learned that this wasn't something that I could step into lightly. I had to go in with the art of command. I had to communicate effectively and make sure that members of staff were trained, developed, and disciplined. The standards, policies, and rules had to be enforced. In the military, we had to maintain a healthy climate. We had to manage resources such as manpower, funds, equipment, facilities, processes, and guidance. We also had to have *process generation*. We had to do this in order to assess how well we were working, a sort of inspection process or program. Our decisions had to be data driven and not personal. We had to make sure that our mission and our vision were compatible with what we were doing. The practice had to be sustainable. It had to have good operational capacity and be strategic. We had to be totally integrated. The military called it total-force integration. This was the best way for all of us to communicate to build this landscape because we had to be immersed in it with boots on the ground. After understanding this second part of the model, you are ready to move to the transitioning phase, the third part of the diagram: energy.

PART 3: ENERGY

This third component of the model came into play for me once I understood the reasons and purpose for what I was doing. I finally understood the legacy part as well as the lay of the land, the language of what was going on. This meant that I could focus on moving forward and taking action. This is where the nitty-gritty of the work takes place. I started implementing the model by approaching doctors and letting them know how I could take their vision for their medical practice and help them incorporate the tools and processes they would need to achieve it.

SIPOC: A Process Improvement Acronym

Supplier: person or organization providing input in a process

Input: resources that are brought to a process by a supplier

Process: series of steps in which an input covers an output

Output: resource that is the result of a process

Customer: person or organization that receives products or services

---

I would use the SIPOC process improvement method to guide my work. I began by evaluating the supplier, and then I looked at the inputs.

Inputs are funding, equipment, and facilities. I ask such questions as:

- How are we going to pay for this?

- Where and how am I going to get it all done?

- The process, the *P* part of SIPOC—how will I execute it?

- How am I going to lead my staff in implementing these tools?

- What kind of process-improvement models are we going to have in place?

Then there is the output. This is the product, the patient care that my business is going to be providing. Then, of course, there are our customers, the *C* part of SIPOC. These are the patients and their families who have to be taken care of. Once we have that, we have our goals in place. The next step is to complete a SWOT analysis. Understanding the SWOT analysis helps formulate a company's business strategy. Then there are metrics, and we make sure that we're monitoring the metrics really closely. We continue to look at opportunities and see if our targets are met, including whether we are seeing enough patients and whether we are able to keep the lights on.

When we see problems, we immediately think of ways to solve them. We look at the problem, the performance gap, the improvement of the target, the value, the stream mapping and analysis, and the root cause analysis, and we learn countermeasures. We then go right back into the metrics to see if our strategy is working.

Energy is the ongoing part. Once you've put the model in place for a medical practice, you still have to make sure what you have established continues to work effectively, including processing, data, optimal patient treatment, and so on. The logistics and back-office structure necessary for a successful private practice still needs to be maintained.

This business model is based on my experiences as a military doctor and what I have learned from those experiences taking care of millions of people in the military, their families, the injured, transiting the entire air-evacuation system, and keeping care constant. This model can be replicated in the civilian world.

Medical practice, or the model of medical practice, has changed. Corporate structure is now necessary for survival. Understanding that and merging corporate structure with consistent, personalized patient care is where the application of my business model comes into play. Through this business model, doctors can wean themselves from the hospital setting and get into their own private practice while not feeling as if they have to cut back on the care that traditional medical practices provide. Physicians are the most highly trained members of the entire medical industry, yet they are nowhere near the top of the power infrastructure or the compensation arena. Insurance executives, hospital executives, and hospital administrators have salaries and bonus compensation packages that far exceed doctors' salaries. The business of medicine and the proliferation of highly paid administrators contribute to the almost $3 trillion of health-care costs. Physicians are surrounded by individuals trained in business in an effort to survive, thus increasing administrative costs and lowering the ever-shrinking profit margin. Some older physicians are choosing to leave, and the loss of institutional memory and experience hurts the entire industry. This is why we providers need to band together and create our own corporate structure in order to survive.

Again, keep in mind that the hospital is not the enemy here. My goal is not to suggest the elimination of hospitals and the very important role that they play. We need hospitals and the wealth of care and technology that they, and the physicians whom they employ, provide. My goal, rather, is for doctors to be able to merge the practice of medicine with business to become their own boss while still being able to provide the best patient care, especially to people in communities where the best medical care can be scarce. Implementing my business model and company's resources will enable doctors to achieve this goal in the same way that I did.

HOW MEDICINE HAS CHANGED

I will attempt to explain why we actually need a corporate structure similar to that of a hospital to sustain a medical practice. Many things have changed in medicine over the years. When I started, I really thought I understood the model of traditional medicine, primary-care providers, doctor-patient relationships, and hospital care. A patient was discharged from a hospital and came back to the primary-care provider to continue treatment. It was a cycle that worked. What has happened recently is that the process has become extremely complicated, and this is why physicians, or I should say, independent physicians, are now being thought of as extinct. To understand this, you've got to understand a couple of things that have occurred. The Affordable Care Act engendered a lot of regulation. I'm going to go through some acronyms to explain this.

NCQA is something that we'll start with: the National Committee for Quality Assurance. The NCQA is an independent 401(k) nonprofit organization in the United States that was set up to improve health care through the administration of evidence-based medicine standards, measures, and programs. It accredits doctors, patients, health plans, policy makers, employers, and any organization across the industry that's involved with patient care. The vendors get certified, software gets certified, and there is compliance auditing. The various health plans can seek accreditation, and their performance can be measured through the administration of what's called HEDIS scores.

HEDIS (healthcare effectiveness data and information set) is the tool used by more than 90 percent of America's health plans to measure performance in important dimensions of care and service, and it's extremely specific. This tool can be used to assess doctors and compare various health plans because metrics that can be measured now exist.

Some of the things they're measuring include asthma control, persistence in using beta-blockers for the treatment of people who've had myocardial infarctions or heart attacks, the control of blood pressure and diabetes, the provision of comprehensive care, breast cancer screening, monitoring patients on antidepressant medications, and assessing the status of childhood and adolescent immunization.

They also measure childhood and adult weight, known as body mass index assessment, and all these factors are compiled to give you a HEDIS score with which to judge the quality of patient care. However, the difficulty in medicine, now, is that primary-care physicians cannot handle all this data. Primary-care physicians are barely getting through the day seeing patients, writing prescriptions, and seeing enough folks so they can balance the books. Doctors need, more or less, to develop a robust practice-management system.

Those are just two of the acronyms, and there are more. There's also what's called CCIP (chronic care improvement program). All the Medicare Advantage organizations must conduct a CCIP as part of their quality improvement.

WHAT ELSE?

STARS is a five-star program they have now implemented for HMOs (health-management organizations), PPOs (preferred-provider organizations), private fee-for-service organizations, and prescription-drug plans. These are also measured with the STARS model.

Then there's PQRS (physician quality reporting system), which encourages individuals, eligible professionals, and group practices to report to Medicare on quality of care. This allows an assessment of the quality of care that physicians and group practices provide, and it's supposed to help ensure that patients get the right care at the right time.

So I'm getting into the "meat and potatoes" to give you an idea of why it is difficult to just manage patients. It's no longer simply about taking care of a simple cold or some abdominal pain.

However, the business of medicine has moved away from the fee-for-service model to the pay-for-performance model. The hospital corporate culture is absolutely not how I have wanted to set up my business model because it sets physicians up for failure. It imposes a negative payment adjustment if the quality measures are not met. There is also a physician fee schedule. Physicians who do not meet these particular metrics have their payments drastically reduced. The overwhelming regulations make some physicians feel they have no choice but to join a large organization, a hospital, or a large group that can pay millions of dollars to have the infrastructure and the staff to crunch these numbers and set up the electronic systems that are required to harvest this data and feed it to the reporting agencies so that they can get paid. That is the environment we now have. When this negative payment adjustment was first established, all of this bureaucracy and chaos resulted in a mass exodus of practicing physicians. In fact, there is still is a mass exodus of older physicians who cannot implement the infrastructure that is needed to handle what is now required.

With my business model, I provide an infrastructure for these vulnerable practitioners to become stable and meet the new rules that govern what I call patient-centered medical care. The benefit of my business model to older physicians is that I come with experience because I have created and utilized this business model once and was able to do it a second time and a third time to expand my practice to eventually combine multiple practices and form a patient-centered medical home (PCMH). I have also proven that it is a scalable model.

In the old days, it was physician and hospital on the top tier, and then the patient was taken care of, or if necessary a patient would be reffered to the hospital to get the care needed, or to another doctor's office. With patient-centered medical care, the patient is at the center of care and outside resources support this. These outside resources include primary-care providers, hospitals, post-acute care, and long-term-care facilities. It also includes clinical-research facilities.

PROVIDER-CENTERED CARE

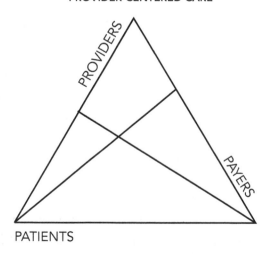

PATIENT-CENTERED CARE

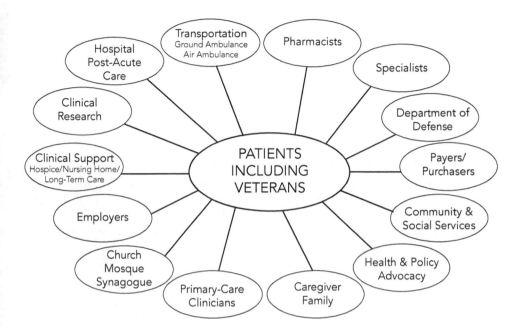

We now include the payers, employers, purchasers and the faith-based organizations because they are helping to influence the care of the patients. You must also consider the patient's family or caregiver, the community, and the social services. Also, the medical specialists, the intensive care unit (ICU) doctors/intensivists, the cardiologists, the pulmonologists, and the oncologists of the hospital must be involved. Finally, we need the government agencies, health and policy advocacy groups, and the US Department of Veterans Affairs (VA).

While the primary physician is trying to manage all of this, it may seem overwhelming. Today's physicians are responsible for organizing all this care, and they are being measured by how their patients are utilizing these resources.

When you finally put this business model into place, you still need to find a way to monitor its progress. This is where I bring in components such as the metrics gap and the constraint analysis. My team and I analyze those findings and look at the opportunities and targets again and go through each component to ensure that the strategies we have implemented are actually working. Consequently, I came up with something that's called a *patient-generation model* because, yes, we have to make sure that we are generating a sustainable patient production average. This patient-generation model tracks the patient-production average. It works like this: There is a minimal number of patients that ensures the profitability of a private practice, but you don't want to make your practice impersonal. It has to be very personable. My formula includes the optimal physician to medical assistant to patient ratio and the number of patients seen during a set period of time. It is individualized for each physician, specific services offered, and the nature of the practice. It lets us know the minimums necessary for the practice to be profitable. That is why, once the model is in place, there's a second layer you need to look at. This is what I call the *trinity of management*.

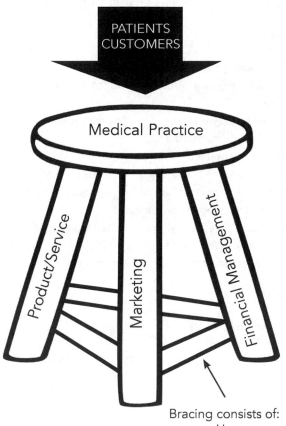

TRINITY OF MANAGEMENT

PATIENTS
CUSTOMERS

Medical Practice

Product/Service

Marketing

Financial Management

Bracing consists of:
Human resources
Risk management
Corporate governance
Product/service quality
Occupational health
Information technology
Policies/procedures
Forms
Processes

This is where we start to look at the *product and the service*. We evaluate whether or not it is working. If it is, we look at marketing and financial management. So, these three components also have to be working well once the system is established: *product-service generation, marketing, and financial management.*

PRACTICE EVALUATION MODEL CHECKLIST

Human Resources

❏ Conflict resolution process implemented
❏ Process for documenting worker's compensation injury implemented
❏ Process for unemployment enquiries implemented
❏ Job descriptions documented
❏ Personnel files maintained
❏ Process for bereavement and celebratory events addressed
❏ Processes for hiring, firing, disciplining, evaluating, training, orienting, and coaching implemented
❏ Personnel policies, wellness programs, pay scales, and job descriptions developed
❏ Process to negotiate/administer benefits developed

Facilities/Equipment

❏ Electronic Health Records system and management implemented
❏ Medical record integrity maintained
❏ Process for handling changes to EHR implemented
❏ EHR Certification by the "Certification Commission for Health Information Technology" obtained
❏ Practice management software integrated with EHR
❏ "Meaningful Use" maintained
❏ Facility is handicap accessible and has met code
❏ "Patient portal" software implemented and easily accessible by patients
❏ Building/suite cleanliness and calm ambience maintained
❏ Ease of parking facilitated
❏ Signage/branding/identity universally applied
❏ Telephones, desktop computers, laptops, iPads, scanners, postage machines, printers, coffee machines, and medical equipment maintained
❏ Vaccine refrigerators, specimen refrigerators, patient refreshment refrigerators, and staff lunch refrigerators maintained (including temperature)

Orders/Expenses

❏ Inventory managed (vaccines, medical consumables, office supplies, kitchen supplies, magazines, business insurance, malpractice insurance, etc.)

❏ Consultant lists maintained—CPA, attorneys, lawn and snow removal service, answering service, water service, plant service, housekeeping, aquarium service, linen service, biohazardous waste removal, shredding service, off-site storage, and courier service contracted.

Legal

❏ Local, state, and federal laws and guidelines adhered to (HIPPA, OSHA, ADA, EOE, FMLA, CLIA, COLA, JCAHO, FACTA, Stark I, II, III, fire safety, disaster communication plan, crash cart and defibrillator maintenance, universal precautions, MSDS hazards, sexual harassment, confidentiality, security, privacy with appropriate documentation to staff, etc.)

❏ Clinical staff licenses: CPR/BLS, ADLS, ATLS maintained

❏ Alternate plan for computer downtime in place

❏ Medical records maintained and released appropriately

Claims/Billing/Accounts Receivable

❏ ICD 10 coding in use and loaded annually; all new RBRVS values loaded

❏ Eligibility searches accomplished on all patients

❏ Dictations/notes completed on all encounters

❏ All payments, denials, and adjustments posted within predetermined time

❏ Electronic claims transmitted daily

❏ Patient claims sent at least weekly (daily is preferable)

❏ Denials appealed

❏ Payer contracts negotiated

❏ All co-pays, co-insurances, and deductibles collected or meeting scheduled with financial counselors

❏ All providers credentialed with all payers

❏ Plan in place for (RAC) Recovery Audit Contractor letters

❏ Monthly reports for provider production, aged accounts receivables, net collection percentages with cost and collections per RVU ran

Accounting

- ❑ Bills paid
- ❑ Payroll produced
- ❑ Compensation schedules for providers prepared
- ❑ Taxes prepared and paid
- ❑ Bank statements reconciled
- ❑ Merchant accounts reconciled
- ❑ Profit and loss statements prepared
- ❑ Refunds to payers and patients prepared
- ❑ Monthly budget and variance reports prepared

Marketing

- ❑ Marketing and research/community outreach performed; new providers introduced to the community
- ❑ Web presence and social media maintained
- ❑ Location and local market analyzed
- ❑ Sponsorship of patient-support groups, local events, sports, and charities initiated
- ❑ Referral sources tracked
- ❑ Media exposure optimized

Operations

- ❑ Clinical data from EHR/clinical decision support simplified
- ❑ Evidence-based medicine performed
- ❑ Team-based practice performed
- ❑ Appointments, including same-day appointments, simplified
- ❑ Chronic care management process enforced
- ❑ Work flow optimized (encounter templates, billing templates, check in, check out, scanned documents,etc.)
- ❑ CMS value-based payment process prepared
- ❑ Operational assessment practiced
- ❑ Resources shared with other providers
- ❑ Behavioral and mental health integrated
- ❑ Consumer support performed
- ❑ Wait times reduced
- ❑ Services menu created and implemented
- ❑ Telemedicine implemented
- ❑ Process for handling prescriptions refills created and enforced

❑ Transcription/scribe services supported
❑ Patient production average/time management optimized
❑ On-call schedule and processes well integrated
❑ Mail opening and recycling solution implemented

Training

❑ Continuing medical education scheduled for clinical staff
❑ Professional membership in organizations maintained
❑ Staff recertification and upgrade training maintained and evaluated (performance reports, medical readiness, training stats, etc,)
❑ Inspection process/metrics/productivity/self-inspection executed

Future/Strategic Planning

❑ New services and locations discussed
❑ Five-year maintenance or growth plan discussed
❑ Financial planning applied (succession plan, retirement plan)
❑ Plan for new provider recruitment implemented
❑ Changing medical landscape forecasted
❑ Projected replacement equipment plan implemented
❑ HEDIS scores (data on patient-reported outcomes) recorded
❑ Path to ACO and MSO association determined
❑ NCQA, PCMH, and PCSP recognition and accreditation obtained

Over time, I made the choice to grow while effectively utilizing my business model. For growth to occur, HR must be robust. You have to make sure you are managing risk well. Corporate governance and the occupational health and safety infrastructure must be intact. IT systems need to be robust. The practice's policies and procedures have to be clear, written out, and adhered to.

In addition, your forms and your process maps have to be totally visible, and you have to make sure that this diagram is adequate. Bracing can't be too loose, or it will not be sustainable. If bracing is too strong, you could end up wasting vital resources. This may cause growth to be limited and even stunted. Therefore, it becomes a balancing act in which each part of the diagram has to be in balance.

Implementing this business model in a medical practice is the most important part of this process. Once you learn the nuts and bolts of each circle or leg of the model and how it can be implemented in your practice, you will begin to reap the benefits of having an autonomous private practice.

Whether this model would be implemented by my company or whether a young physician were to implement it on his/her own, he/she would still need to have certain policies established. For starters, a good IT system would have to be in place with good practice- management software and EMRs. Appropriate workflow processes would also be necessary.

These are not new things to a young physician looking to be an entrepreneur. They can, however, be a little overwhelming. My team and I would meet extensively with the doctor in charge of the private practice to demonstrate how to get patient production average optimized so as to best manage time. I would assess the inventory that may be needed and the kind of practice management and inventory management necessary for supplies, vaccines, and medication. I would evaluate the office's storage and labeling, and so on. The evaluation at this point would involve using the initial criterion for evaluating a practice for purchase discussed in chapter 4. However, at this point, we become even more specific.

Some other factors that I look at when evaluating the private-practice improvement process are:

1. **Ambience:** Is the office clean and friendly?

2. **Work flow:** Is it clean and efficient and without bottlenecks?

3. **Equipment:** Is it working and up to date?

The checklist I maintain for each evaluation of a private practice includes revisiting, re-evaluating and continuing to ask such questions as:

- ✓ Does the practice have ancillary services?
- ✓ Is the office's answering service up to date, and is it easy for patients to call the office?
- ✓ Are the office's Occupation Safety and Health Administration (OSHA) requirements up to date?
- ✓ Does the office offer telemedicine services?
- ✓ What kind of signage is on the building?
- ✓ Is the office located in an area that's being gentrified? Is it in a location that's growing or stagnant?
- ✓ Is there enough ventilation in the practice?
- ✓ Who provides the cleaning services for the office, and are they reliable?

Continue to implement the improvement-process plan loop. Always ask questions and strive to improve.

Then, I move on to the HR department and begin asking the following:

- ✓ Who is managing human resources?
- ✓ Who is doing the marketing?
- ✓ Who is managing the metrics and the productivity?
- ✓ Who's doing the credentialing?
- ✓ Who is teaching the staff to use technology meaningfully?
- ✓ What about payroll, accounting, helping with prescriptions, and patient documentation?
- ✓ Who is helping set up NCQA certification and recognition?
- ✓ Who is helping with the customer assessment of health-care provider systems?

The next thing would be the CCIP. Practice staff need to be well informed about this program and know who is working as the liaison to establish it. Who's helping with the quality improvement process (QIP)? You must have a physician-quality reporting system in place. So if you're going to be an independent practitioner with no help, all these things would have to be ironed out before you could even see your first patient.

This preparation for growth is where my model would work as a franchise: my company would help to overhaul and then manage your practice. This would all be in an effort to make the practice more efficient and profitable for you, the doctor, and your patients. Again, my goal is for doctors, or providers, to have options regarding the future of their private practice. I would discuss with the doctors, or providers, what currently works and what does not work well in their business and what they may need to get rid of. Some strategies, paperwork, and so on, might need to be discarded. Paper charts, for example, would need to be removed so the practice could move toward a paperless system. For all medical records, we would have to do chart management—scanning records into an electronic medical record and setting up practice-management software. My team could train doctors and their staff to set up EMRs for all of their patients or completely revamp their infrastructure. We are capable of doing whatever is necessary to streamline operations

IMPLEMENTATION OPTIONS

Option one: If doctors want to do all that I just mentioned on their own, they will find that the project is not do-it-yourself. They will still need assistance and constant consultation with my company. I would give them the basics of what needs to be done, and they could maybe figure it out after that, armed with tools they would not have gotten anywhere else. However, they would still be on their own, and they would not have the expertise of my team of business people built into the practice's infrastructure to enable them to succeed in implementing this model. I have not seen tools anywhere else that provide instruction on implementation, but if you need somebody to crawl on and under desks to make sure your IT system works properly, our team will come in and help you do that.

Here are the three things that Kingdom Medicine, PA, offers:

We are available for consultation. This is where we come in and help you "fix up" your practice to set you up for success. We can do this, and then we would be available for further consultation if necessary.

We manage your services. Instead of employing the multitude of staff you normally need to run a practice, you can hire us as a management-service organization.

We become an employer. We employ you: we take over your practice, and we build it out, and you become part of our team of experts. This option is the franchise model.

Therefore, with my model, if you allow me to help you, we can create a turnkey model for a practice in which you can remain independent. We can either employ you—your practice will become one of our facilities located in a specific area that's in need—or you can have your own facility, and we will become the management service for that organization. It is as simple as that. Once you have gotten all of these things in line, you are ready to see the success of your entrepreneurship and strategic decision making take flight.

I have broken down the steps that must be followed and listed them below:

STEPS TO INDEPENDENT PRACTICE

Step 1: Graduate from medical school and obtain a state medical license.

Step 2: Obtain a tax ID number, drug enforcement administration (DEA) number, controlled dangerous substance (CDS) number, and national provider identifier (NPI) number.

Step 3: Determine if it is a solo, group, or hospital practice. Request credentialing from insurance companies.

Step 4: Lease or purchase space, hire staff, and obtain hospital privileges.

Step 5: Choose robust, certified EMRs and practice-management systems. EMRs should be certified by the Department of Health and Human Services (HHS), as the Certification Commission for Health Information Technology (CCHIT) was the certification used in the past and is becoming obsolete. This has resulted in the American Recovery and Reinvestment Act (ARRA) of 2009 formalizing the role and responsibility of the Office of the National Coordinator for Health Information Technology (ONCHIT) within the Department of HHS.

Step 6: Start seeing patients.

Step 7: Meet meaningful use, patient-centered medical home certification (PCMH), physician quality reporting system (PQRS), and National Committee for Quality Assurance (NCQA) accreditations.

Step 8: Participate in managed care organization (MCO); continue to build infrastructure.

Step 9a: Partner with physician accountable-care organizations (ACOs). Each ACO has to cover a minimum of five thousand Medicare beneficiaries for at least three years.

Or,

Step 9b: Partner with hospital accountable-care organizations. ACOs are groups of doctors, hospitals, and other health-care providers that come together voluntarily to give coordinated, high-quality care to their patients. The goal is to ensure that patients, especially chronically ill, get the right care at the right time while avoiding unnecessary duplication of services and preventing medical errors. This leads to improved quality and increased patient satisfaction at lower cost.

Step 10: Develop your ground game. This involves a robust preventative-care program, customer support, customized patient experience, enhanced population health management, data sets and analytics, behavioral health programs, optimized end-of-life management, chronic care management, transitional-care management strategies, patient portal with bidirectional input for patient optimization, bundled contracts with payers, and managed high-risk patients.

Step 11: Reset expectations. Partner with home-health providers, nursing homes, and hospitals. Develop revenue sharing/shared-savings infrastructure and formulas. Reduce waste. Improve quality. Close points of leakage, and reduce duplicity of costs. Develop a clinically integrated network. Steer patients back to the team. Recognize the value of keeping patients out of the emergency room. Manage performance and strategic expansion.

Step 12: Ensure that value-based payment modifier (VBPM) methodology is implemented with a process-ensuring transition to the Medicare Access and CHIP Reauthorization Act (MACRA).

*Steps 9a and 9b represent two possible paths. Steps 10 and 11 would be accomplished with either a physician-owned ACO or a hospital-owned ACO. I personally prefer the physician **ACO**, as this allows the physicians to maintain autonomy and reap the benefits of a large group.

BECOMING AN INDEPENDENT PRACTITIONER

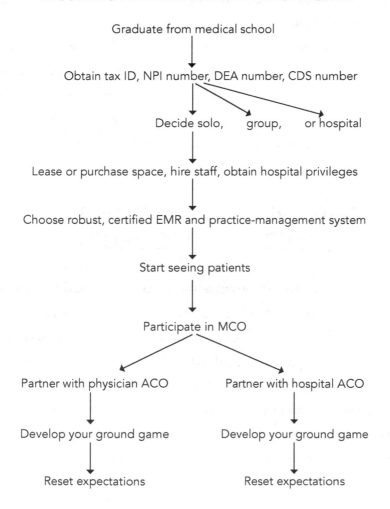

In chapter 4, I mentioned that when I was in the first stage of developing my business model and shared it with my colleagues, I experienced a lot of pushback from them. They were my loudest opposition. Today I have proven to myself and my peers that my idea (turned business model) has worked. Those loud naysayers almost deterred me from accomplishing my dream of success in medicine. Nonetheless, I did not hate them for it or become bitter toward them. Instead, I used their doubts and negativity as fuel for my fire. At the time, my ideas were new to them and unorthodox. They couldn't picture how merging traditional medicine, technology, and business could actually work.

Physicians are retiring at an alarming rate—literally, walking out of their practices. I have been told about not just one physician, but up to four physicians in my particular area who just walked away from their practices because no one was buying them. Moreover, I am now being contacted by doctors who want to implement my business model

THE SHIFT TO ELECTRONIC MEDICAL RECORDS

When I created this business model and then used it, I did so through knowledge and experience, even when many people around me thought I was crazy. I knew that the integration of electronic records in private practice would work. When I was in the military in 1997, the military already had EMRs, and the VA already had them. I was exposed to this technology while doing a rotation when I was in medical school. First, I did some rotations in the VA, and then again, when I went into the military, I was exposed to EMRs.

At that time you had no choice. You were told what to do, and you were told the information went into an EMR. It was very different and difficult at first, but you got used to it pretty quickly. When I started my own practice, I started it with EMRs. I went out and spoke to vendors and started using EMRs off the bat at a time when most physicians were not using them. This was in 2000. Their use put me ahead of the curve. I didn't start with paper charts and then switch to EMR technology. Instead, I started with it. My colleagues only started using EMRs when they were mandated to do so by the government and by the insurance companies and payers.

Around 2013, the government began giving doctors incentives to use EMRs. By the time this happened, I was about twelve years ahead of the curve. I saw the transition from the old EMRs to the newer ones, and when doctors and hospitals needed them, EMRs started to be regulated. Before the government stepped in and created regulation and the use of EMRs grew in popularity, companies were creating them and charging an arm and a leg for this technology. It was like the Wild West. When the government got involved, the EMR companies were required to meet certain standards, and a lot of EMR products fell by the wayside. However, by then I had a thorough understanding of the technology, so it didn't hinder me. All I had to do was transfer data from one electronic system to the next. To meet the measures that were required, the metrics, the NCQAs and the HEDIS measures, and so forth, it was easier for me because I already had all the data in electronic format.

THE ELECTRONIC ADVANTAGE

The use of EMRs became the sustaining part of my model and it remains so. The front office is where patients are seen, and the back office is where the infrastructure is: the phones, the faxes—none of that is in front. Therefore, being able to handle all this patient data in electronic format is a strategic advantage. If you have six thousand patients' records in an electronic format, you have access to that data immediately. If you've taken the time to build out that data, then, at the click of a button, you have instant access to it.

While patients are describing their symptoms ("Oh, this is what's going on. I'm having a cold. I'm having fevers."), I do a quick exam, then simply go to the computer, click on "pharmacy," type in the medication I want, and then click on "send." I make a quick note, and I am all done. This process has now increased efficiency and accessibility. But the back office is something different. I developed the back office because of the massive amount of requirements imposed on doctors.

With all of those requirements and the requirement to meet meaningful use—which is another way of measuring and monitoring—I needed additional staff. If I were to do that in the office, it would necessitate more build-out, and I would have lots of staff running around. So, rather than sitting in the space where we have patients and receptionists and nurses and medical assistants, my administrative staff members sit in a place where they do not interrupt the flow of the clinical staff. Hence, they occupy the back office. By moving them to a different space and using economies of scale, I now have that same staff handle one practice, two practices, three practices—I build that back office to meet the need of the front offices.

As you can see, I don't have to duplicate the entire thing. I don't have to build the record-management section three times or four times or five times. It just needs to be built once. As a result, I'm saving on lease space, I'm saving on administrative expenses and manpower, and I'm saving on staff.

This setup, however, does not disregard the corporate structure and its influence on the success of the business. With my business model, I still use the power of that corporate structure, but the advantage to my model is that patient care is not hindered because doctors' pay is not based on how well the doctors fit into that structure. It is not a bonus-pay structure. The advantage here is the intimacy the patients benefit from. When patients come to the practice, they are not lost in a huge bureaucracy of paperwork and regulations. The bureaucracy does exist, but it is not right in front of them, which means they are not distracted. The bureaucracy is also removed from the physicians' immediate surroundings because it's being taken care of in the background, where it's not seen.

Think of it as a duck floating on a pond. Things are calm on the surface, but there's a lot of paddling going on underwater. In the hospital you don't see that. The hospital is a totally different entity. We will always need the hospital because it is a part of the patient-centered care group; however, a large hospital can't be a small practice. We need the efficiency of a hospital corporate structure in a small-patient setting to be effective. The hospitals have tried but have not been able to duplicate that model because they do it from the top down. They don't understand how to be intimate with the patient in the small-practice setting. That is the difference between building it from the ground up versus mandating from the top down. Hospitals are buying practices and telling employed doctors how they want them to practice medicine. There is no real relationship developed with the patients, but these same patients are now owned by the hospital.

When the hospital takes over a physician's practice, it gains all the patients. If the hospital and the physician part ways, the physician leaves with no patients. The patients now belong to the hospital. *The difference in my business model is that you, the physician, will have an intimate relationship with those patients because we're helping you manage your practice.* We're helping you retain your independence if that's what you want to do. Now, if you're an older physician, and you want to eventually retire and now simply want to be employed instead of focusing on the practice administration, we can also do that for you.

We give you a W-2, the form that an employer must send to an employee and the Internal Revenue Service, and we pay you. We take over the management, and it's all without your having to deal with the stress of overhead and practice management, and you will still be well compensated as you meet the new quality measures. The main advantage is that the intimacy of care that's not provided in the hospital can still be provided in a small medical practice. You also have the option to be independent if you want, to use a consultant if you want, or to be employed if you want, with a retirement option. My business model allows the physician to maintain his or her dignity with some autonomy.

Moreover, I want to also put young doctors in control. Young doctors with entrepreneurial minds should be able to apply my business model to achieve success in their medical practices.

PEARL #6:
Successful people generally
have two things in common:
sustained focus and persistence.

CHAPTER 7

THE ROAD TO SUCCESS

I'm here to build something for the long term.
Anything else is a distraction.
—Mark Zuckerberg

J ohn Maxwell, a famous author, speaker, and pastor who has written many books focused primarily on leadership, can easily be labeled as the one of the foremost authorities on leadership and personal development. He once said, "Leadership is not about titles, positions, or flowcharts. It is about one life influencing another." I would say that Mr. Maxwell was very likely speaking from experience when he made this statement. Many people, such as Dale Carnegie, author of *How to Win Friends and Influence People*, have influenced John Maxwell's life and successes so that he could, in turn, do the same for people like me.

My road to success—from my achievements in track and field while in high school and attending the Pan-American Games to my emigration from the Caribbean to the United States to attend college and medical school, joining the USAF, completing my residency, beginning my hospital career, opening my own private practice, and now entrepreneurship—stemmed from the wisdom I learned from the people who went before me.

It can always be said that there is wisdom in learning from those who have gone before you. They have made their mistakes, experienced disappointments, and rejoiced in the successes that have made them who they are. Inevitably, through their experiences, they have paved the way for the rest of us to achieve the same successes, and then some. We stand on their shoulders as we reach for our own dreams. And what strong and worthy shoulders those are.

The first shoulders I stood on were my father's. He taught me my first lessons in life. He was my first hero. His lessons about perseverance, hope, love, faith, dedication, and success are lessons that I am still learning today. Some other heroes I admire include:

Foot soldier from Earl of Dunmore's Ethiopian Regiment. Charcoal illustration by Leonard Richardson M.D.

- **Earl of Dunmore's Ethiopian Regiment (1775):** Five thousand black soldiers served as patriots during the Revolutionary War. They fought mostly in integrated units and were critical in battles on Rhode Island, Long Island, Red Bank, Savannah, Monmouth, and Fort Griswold. One-third of General Schuyler's army was African American. On July 9, 1775, George Washington directed colonial recruiters to not enlist "any deserter from the ministerial army, nor any stroller, black or vagabond, or persons suspected of being an enemy to the liberty of America." George Washington's Adjutant General ordered that African Americans were no longer to be recruited or allowed to reenlist in the Continental Army. This resolution was approved by the Continental Congress on October 23. On November 7, John Murray, the British governor of Virginia, freed all African Americans willing to serve under the British flag. Thousands of former slaves put on British uniforms and fought gallantly for King George IV. They included the Earl of Dunmore's Ethiopian Regiment, formed in 1775, Black Empire Loyalists formed in 1776, and the West Norfolk 54th Regiment (a.k.a. Black Pioneers), also formed in 1776. Alarmed by the changing events, George Washington reversed his decision on December 31 and reinstituted enlistment of African Americans into the Continental Army.

- **Fifth West Indian Regiment (1814–1815):**
The British Army employed regiments of all-black soldiers—namely, the First West Indian Regiment and the Fifth West Indian Regiment. The Fifth West Indian Regiment saw action at the battle of the West Bank. In all, there were twelve regiments of black soldiers raised to garrison British possessions in the Caribbean.

Fifth West Indian Regiment foot soldier. Charcoal illustration by Leonard Richardson, MD

- **Ninth and Tenth Calvary Units (1867):**
Congress approved the first African American cavalry units. Commanded by white officers and operating under intense disadvantages, they developed into remarkable fighting units during their extensive engagements on the southern plains. Called

many names, most of which were insulting, they adopted the name given to them by their Indian opponents, "Buffalo Soldiers," a title of which they were proud.

Gen Benjamin O Davis, Jr. Charcoal illustration by Leonard Richardson, MD

• **Colonel Benjamin Oliver Davis Jr. and the Tuskegee Airmen (1942):** On March 7, the first cadets graduated from flying school at Tuskegee and received commissions in the US Air Corp. On October 13, the 332nd Fighter Group was activated. Colonel Benjamin O. Davis Jr. became the commander of the 99th Pursuit Squadron. They were attached to the 33rd Fighter Group and were stationed in North Africa. In 1943, the 477th Bomber Group

Red Tail P-51 Mustang flown by Tuskegee Airman pilot over Italy. Oil on canvas by Leonard Richardson M.D.

was formed. The Tuskegee airmen flew their first combat missions, strafing enemy positions on the heavily fortified Italian island of Pantelleria. On January 3, 1944, they entered the war in Europe and contributed to the critical mission of bomber escort.

• **General Lloyd ("Fig") Newton (1974):** He was the first African American pilot to fly with the elite USAF Air Demonstration Squadron, the Thunder Birds. He went on to become one of the few four-star generals in the USAF.

General Lloyd ("Fig") Newton with various aircraft flown including the Lockheed F-117 Nighthawk in the foreground. Charcoal illustration by Leonard Richardson, MD

- **General Daniel ("Chappie") James Jr. (1995):** He was the first African American promoted to the rank of four-star general in the USAF and named commander in chief of the North American Air Defense Command.

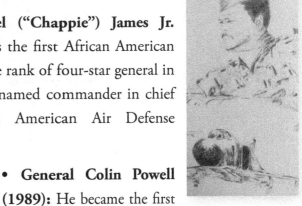

General Daniel ("Chappie") James Jr. with McDonnell Douglas F-4 phantom II. Charcoal illustration by Leonard Richardson, MD

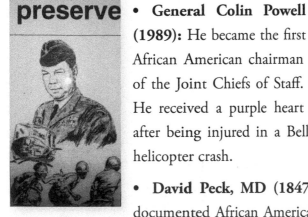

Gen. Colin Powell. Art featured in "Hilltop Times Charcoal illustration by Leonard Richardson, MD

- **General Colin Powell (1989):** He became the first African American chairman of the Joint Chiefs of Staff. He received a purple heart after being injured in a Bell Vietnam era Huey helicopter crash.

- **David Peck, MD (1847):** He was the first documented African American graduate of a US medical school, Rush Medical College in Chicago. He was a prominent abolitionist and minister who founded the local AME Church of Carlisle.

- **James McCune Smith, MD (1837):** He was the first African American to earn a medical degree in 1837. Rejected from US medical schools, he attended the University of Glasgow, Scotland.

James McCune Smith, MD. Source: US National Library of Medicine, National Institutes of Health.

- **Major Martin Robinson Delany (1863):** He was the first and highest-ranking African American commissioned field grade officer of the Union Army. President Lincoln referred to the Harvard-trained officer as "the most extraordinary and intelligent black

Maj. Martin Delany. Oil on canvas by Leonard Richardson M.D.

man." He was a physician, editor, lecturer, writer, and antislavery activist.

- **Alexander Augusta, MD (1863–1864):** He was a Civil War surgeon who headed Freedmen's Hospital in Washington, DC. He was also the first African American to receive a medical commission in the US Army and went on to become the highest-ranking of the 111 commissioned African American officers.

Alexander Augusta, M.D.
Source: en.wikipedia.org

Vance Marchbanks, M.D
Source: nellis.af.mil

- **Vance Marchbanks, MD (1941):** He was commissioned as the surgeon for the 332nd Fighter Group (Tuskegee Airmen) and for Tuskegee Army Air Force Base. He was a NASA flight surgeon, space medical pioneer, and colonel in the USAF. He was appointed project physician for Project Mercury, the first manned US space flight.

- **Marion Mann, MD, PhD (1975):** He became the first MD general in the US Army and was Commander of the 229th US Army General Hospital.

- **Sir Cuthbert M. Sebastian (1940s–present):** He is a private practitioner, hospital administrator, doctor of medicine and master of surgery, ob-gyn,

Marion Mann, M.D., PhD.
Source: Book; African American Medical Pioneers. TASO army photo facility, Fort Mead, MD

Dr. Sir Cuthbert M. Sebastian GCMG OBE MDCM
Source: jayblessed.com

doctor of the prisons—police and army, chief medical officer, Governor General of St. Kitts and Nevis, author, statesman, and mentor to an entire generation.

Charles Drew, M.D.
Source: counter-currents.com

• **Charles Drew, MD (1940):** I spoke about him in the book's introduction. Dr. Drew organized a blood bank to supply plasma to the British. In 1941, he directed the first American Red Cross blood bank.

There are the "shoulders" of institutions, such as Howard University College of Medicine, which led the way in training physicians of African descent. Major General Howard and others started Howard University and Howard University College of Medicine back in 1867 and 1868, respectively, with the goal of uplifting African Americans, especially those recently released from slavery. A secondary goal was to help prevent disease among the newly freed slaves from entering the white population. They said, "If we train black physicians, they can treat black patients. That would prevent disease from traveling to the white population." At the time, there were a lot of newly freed slaves. The hospital was called Freedmen's Hospital, and they named Howard University after General Howard. General Oliver O. Howard was a major general who served on the Union side in the American

Major General Oliver O. Howard. Source: Library of Congress

Civil War. He helped found Howard University, where he served as president for several years. This school and hospital were the official start of organized medicine for larger groups of African Americans in the United States and were responsible for training the largest group of African American physicians. I was able to be a part of that history by attending that university. Howard was instrumental in the type of physician I became and instrumental in my being able to learn about myself. Even though I was accepted to other medical institutions, I thought that Howard University was both historical and powerful, as I was also learning about my legacy.

These are the driving and sustaining forces from hundreds of years ago to the present that have allowed me to be where I am today. I am proud that I have been able to stand on the shoulders of these giants who went before me. The only way that you can grow, be successful, even learn to set goals and implement them is by understanding those who have gone before you, who have paved the way for you to be who you are.

RESULTS OF GOAL SETTING

When you make a decision to go after your dreams, armed with the lessons you have learned from those who have paved the way for you, you will quickly realize the importance of goal setting. Now you can practice medicine in the way you want to practice it and be successful in business while keeping the traditional model of medicine—and goal setting is what gets you there.

From day one, I knew what I wanted to achieve in life and in my career. And I knew what others had done before me to give me the opportunity to become a physician. As a result, I saw medicine and medical practice in a whole new light. The goal that I set was to be a successful physician—and success for me, at that time, meant independence. It meant financial security. It meant the ability to help those who couldn't help themselves. It meant being able to provide for my family, and it meant a comfortable retirement.

So, I set that goal, and when I went into the hospital and started practicing hospital medicine, I attempted to learn the trade from the perspective of an attending physician. I soon realized that I couldn't just hang out my shingle and be successful, especially when I had to pay back medical-school loans. I needed to have a sustainable income that could take care of all my expenses.

I recognized that building a medical practice would take time. Therefore, I planned a ten-year course of action in which I would not depend on anyone but myself and my maker. My definition of success did not change from what it was originally. My definition remained the same, with an emphasis on the freedom to, basically, do what I wanted to do when I wanted to do it. Working in the hospital for someone else meant that I could make a decent wage but would end up being a slave to the system. Somebody in charge would always be telling me when I could and could not work. So, again, independence became the main pillar in my definition of success. Independence would gain me financial security, control of my time, and full autonomy.

This is why you must have a set of goals to accomplish your success. It is absolutely paramount that you have a goal and a timeline. Remember one of the pearls I shared: "There is no progress without action." Well, action is what needs to take place for you to make progress in your goals. Goals are meant to be acted on. And having a time limit helps because it allows your sustained focus to materialize. Since you have a goal, you can't put off until tomorrow what can be done today. Something as involved as medicine helps keep you focused on what you need to do.

OUT WITH THE OLD

When you have set a goal to be financially sound through your medical practice, you may need to get rid of some old systems and implement new ones in their place. As I pursued my goals, I realized that medicine is much more complex than I had originally thought. With government mandates, payer demands, disgruntled patients who didn't understand exactly what the physician was dealing with and what it took to maintain their medical records, I recognized that I had to manage the complexity of practicing medicine. Among other things, I turned to professional medical societies for ideas on how to do it. I talked to peers, went to seminars on training, and so forth to figure out what was the best way forward.

In doing so, however, I discovered that information for the independent entrepreneurial physician was somewhat limited. The trend was toward employment of physicians by large, managed-care organizations and hospitals. Yes, physician employees are able to make a decent living, but that was not what I had in mind. It meant losing autonomy, which, for me, would not have been success.

These shortcomings led me to figure out how I could become an independent physician. How could I go back to the old-fashioned ways of practicing medicine? I figured out that if I could have economies of scale, if I could use technology, if I could use cloud-based systems and services, I could create a system that would allow me to practice medicine as a solo provider. That was how I would meet my goal.

I have attained that success. I have created new patterns and new ways of enforcing my business strategy and medical model. In order to achieve success, you more than likely cannot continue the same routine. You must be open and ready to change, learn, and be vulnerable. In expanding your personal vision, you must see yourself accomplishing it and being victorious in it.

Because the medical community is a diverse set of individuals, I had to come up with a flexible plan. I recognized that with the changes in medicine—for example, nurse practitioners becoming independent primary-care providers—I could not just focus on young doctors. I also had to consider nurse practitioners and PAs who could "hang out their shingle"—meaning to open a private practice—if they had an entrepreneurial mind and could adopt an entrepreneurial business model. I wanted to talk to them, encourage them, and show them how, together, we could reclaim the patient/physician relationship.

Incidentally, I realized that this way of thinking was limited to one segment of the medical community. What about those physicians who needed help stabilizing their vulnerable practices? They also represented a market. I could come in and show them how to stabilize their practice. I also recognized that not only did younger doctors have the entrepreneurial spirit but so did older doctors who needed help in succession planning because they were looking at retirement.

Therefore, the model that I came up with encompasses not only young physicians but also those physicians who are right in the middle. They are halfway through their journey, and maybe they are having trouble stabilizing their volume of practice, or they may be older and thinking about retirement, or they may be nurse practitioners. All these professionals can benefit from this business model I've created.

This was where my original vision had expanded. I was not just talking to one individual anymore. I was now talking to the entire medical community and saying, "This is where you can fit! We must reclaim the patient-physician relationship, and this is how you can have some autonomy and independence so that you can find the best place for you."

PEARL #7:

Whatever you hope to achieve, you can.
With enough determination and planning,
anything is possible.

CHAPTER 8

THE FUTURE OF
MEDICINE

*To raise new questions, new possibilities, to regard
old problems from a new angle, requires creative
imagination and marks real advance in science.*
—Albert Einstein

I f we follow in the footsteps of Leonardo da Vinci and Jules
Verne, we may get a chance to look into the future and
determine what the future of medicine may be. The question
is whether I believe that medicine has a bright future. Most of our
vision of the future can be extrapolated from current technologies
that exist today, such as robot surgeons.

This future already exists in some sort of rudimentary form. In fact, there's a field of study called string field theory, or general string theory. It draws on current research and it shows, based on what's happening now, what the future is going to look like. So, in a sense, the future has already been written.

On the horizon, we can look forward to bloodless surgery, cryopreservation, an HIV vaccine, an Ebola vaccine, nanoparticle technology, anticancer immunotherapies, robotic surgery advances, biomarkers for disease, antighrelin therapies, xeno transplantation, an artificial pancreas, 3D organ printing, and anti-aging therapy.

What I see in the future is based on what exists now, combined with my own conclusions. I've followed the research of biologist Leroy Hood. He talks about *P4 medicine:* predictive, personalized, preventive, and participatory medicine, to which I add: point of care, precision, and empowering bright brains.

Essentially, we have roughly seven billion humans on the planet, each of whom is different. Even though we have the same DNA, the interaction between the environment and our lifestyles, as well as family predisposition to disease, immune status, and susceptibility to diseases affects the way in which we become sick.

In the future, rather than running tests based on averages, we will use an individual's specific DNA data to prescribe therapy specifically targeted to that individual. We will know which genes will be turned on in which organs. We can then counsel patients on their specific lifestyles and diets and treatments. Their DNA will allow treatments to be predictive and more personalized. We will be able to predict through DNA, diseases and conditions to which a patient is prone. We will then be able to practice preventative medicine. This will revolutionize the way patients are treated.

Patients are going to be very involved in their own health-care decisions, aiding in patient empowerment. Patients will have wearable devices or implantable devices that give real-time data so that seniors can live healthier and longer lives.

I also see patients helping patients. I see doctors providing group visits for people with similar conditions. I see more caregiver engagement. Care is going to be better coordinated. Instead of being disease centered, care will be more patient centered.

We are going to focus more on wellness programs, keeping people healthy. We're going to focus more on population health, with populations monitored closely, and doctors will be judged on how they take care of the entire population. Care is going to be community based. We are going to have exercise programs at work and more initiatives for keeping people healthy.

Again, talking about bright brains, innovation is going to be streamlined. We are going to have nanomedicine and nanotechnology. For example, anticancer drugs are going to be hidden in these nanoshells, and specific cancer cells will be targeted much more accurately than they are with the standard chemotherapy we now use. We will make great use of surgeon robotics. A surgeon, through robotic technology, will be able to provide surgery in another part of the country, another part of the world, from the place in which he is physically located.

We will have new ways to see things using technology such as the pill cam, a tiny pill that's actually a camera and is able to film the entire GI tract as it travels through the gut. Technology will reduce costs. In addition, testing is going to be less invasive. Pharmacology will be targeted more to prevention. Treatment will be based on guided prescribing, in which the doctor looks at DNA—for example,

BRCA1 or BRCA2 genes, or neuroreceptors. Doctors will also focus on preventative therapy and prophylactic therapy.

There are also going to be advances in microfluidics and micro-electronics. Alao, importantly, the cost will go down for genome sequencing. The Human Genome Project costs about 2.7 billion dollars over a thirteen-year span to complete a high-quality version of the human DNA sequence. In just a few years, I believe it will cost a lot less—perhaps a few thousand dollars to map entire genomes for single individuals and completing hundreds in one day. We will all have our own biological DNA template. We will then be able to forecast the treatment that individual patients need. We will be able to continuously monitor the body's systems, which will allow us to identify illnesses earlier and thus treat them more effectively. The National Human Genome Research Institute's genetic-variation mapping projects allow rapid discovery of genes related to common illnesses such as asthma, diabetes, heart disease, and cancer.

As a medical community, we're going to empower bright minds. Right now, it takes time to put a great idea into practice. There will be a fast track to help people with brilliant ideas get their innovations out. Innovation will enjoy strong support.

This will all, without a doubt, involve a coming together and working together of hospitals and independent medical practices. We will have no choice but to be seamless when doing this, because the patient will be of utmost importance—not the hospital, not the doctor. It's going to be our job to make sure that patients get what they need. The future of medicine will mean that patients will have control of their EMR data, which has been held hostage by some vendors. Right now, the VA utilizes a technology called the blue button option, giving patients access to their records. This is going to be universal. Vendors are going to be forced to open up the systems.

Patients are going to have control of their medical records and use that information however they see fit. If they want information about what they're prone to, that information will be made available to them at their request.

I believe we have now entered the era of the empowered patient. Just as the cell phone is now part of a patient's wardrobe or the smartphone is an accessory, so will health technology be. Patients will then have everything at their fingertips. The land-line phone will no longer keep them hostage. The cell phone will now work for them. This is my vision of what is going to happen with health care. It will work for the patient, and physicians will serve them as originally intended.

Between 1963 and 2010, we have had few cures for illnesses such as heart disease, Parkinson's disease, and cancer. However, we now have the ability to reduce the heart disease death rate by 76 percent. We have a new treatment for prostate cancer and chronic myelogenous leukemia (CML). We have increased options for multiple sclerosis (MS), Parkinson's, and human immunodeficiency virus (HIV), and with the emergence of gene therapy and germline therapy, we now have the ability to edit nature's software with gene drives such as CRISPR and genome editing. The question is no longer "Can it be done?" but rather,

- "Is it ethical?"

- "Who is responsible for the decision making?"

- "How will we alter the shared environment?"

- "Do we understand the repercussions of genetic intervention?"

- "What if we remove from the world the mosquito that spreads zika, dengue and malaria, the black fly that spreads river blindness, bats that harbor ebola, mice that harbor lime disease? Will we realize too late that they served another valuable purpose?"

Armed with information and armed with technology, medical practice is now redefined as whatever you want it to be. The doctor who can meet new patients where they are and provide what they need—whether it's telehealth, whether it's global medicine, whether it's medical tourism, or whether it's providing them with a copy of their DNA and genomic sequence—will be the doctor who is practicing medicine of the future.

THE GLOBAL FUTURE
OF MEDICINE

Furthermore, I see the future of medicine going overseas. My goal is to implement my successful business model across the United States, simply because there are people who are still not getting adequate care. As mentioned earlier, my model allows doctors to go into communities where people are not being treated and meeting them where they are. This is an area where telehealth could flourish— for example, teleradiology would allow for difficult and sophisticated imaging studies to be interpreted at a remote location, and telepsychiatry could end the shortage of psychiatrists. Because I understand the Caribbean, I also have a place in my heart to reach out to patients there as well. When my father became sick, he did not have access in St. Kitts or Anguilla to the medical technologies that we have in the United States. I can envision how my business model can be utilized there. There are many physicians here in the United States, and some are of Caribbean ancestry. I believe Caribbean governments should invest in two or three tertiary-level centers, maybe in Jamaica, Trinidad, and Barbados. Each would specialize in one particular area, and we could maintain a fleet of air ambulances, which, incidentally, coincides with my training in aerospace medicine and air ambulances.

My vision and strategy would be to equip the smaller islands with good telecommunication systems so the specialists can talk to the general practitioners, the general surgeons, and guide them through any difficult procedures that may need to be done. This could be done at a fraction of the current cost that is incurred when patients try to treat themselves or fly to Miami to get care.

In the Caribbean, my business model would change ever so slightly because we are dealing with geographical boundaries such as the Caribbean Sea and the Atlantic Ocean. We would have to devise methods to get the patients to where they could be seen effectively. As mentioned earlier, this would involve a model that's used in the military for aerospace medicine; air evacuations; and primary, secondary, and tertiary centers. I visualize building two or three tertiary centers around the Caribbean. I visualize a fleet of air ambulances. I visualize a system of well-coordinated primary and secondary centers that could triage patients and get them to where they need to be treated effectively.

I visualize this being done in a sustainable way that is cost effective. It would, however, involve buy-in from local governments. It would involve investing in the infrastructure and in the population, and it would involve a reeducation of what's possible because if you don't think it can happen, then it's not going to happen. People in places such as the smaller Caribbean Islands have to stop thinking that patients have to go abroad to get the best care. There are already brilliant minds there. We just have to unleash those minds and let them function where they are. West Indians already contribute a significant amount to medicine here in the United States, with so many physicians, nurses, nurse practitioners and PAs being of West Indian descent. Coupled with the brilliant minds already existing in the Caribbean, all we need is the infrastructure to take care of our own patient population.

Once the infrastructure is in place in the Caribbean, it would help the family practice doctor who is located deep in the country-side. The community benefits from a network of providers to whom we could say, "This physician over in this region is looking at retirement or needs a vacation. Are you willing to go there and fill in? Here is an opportunity for you to start your own practice."

It also fosters economies of scale. Overseas doctors would get their medicines at a reduced price, delivered to them. They would buy whatever they needed for their practice at the best rate possible because they could buy in bulk, and my team would deliver it. In addition, we would help those doctors answer the phones and set up scheduling. We would have someone covering for them. With modern technology, the medical practice could be set up anywhere at any time with the support of an entire infrastructure, which is cloud based or Internet based. For example, let's say that we have hundreds of employees. That single practice in Sandy Point, Saint Kitts, or East End, Anguilla, could now have hundreds of people literally working for that doctor. If that doctor needs logistics, pharmacy services, or HR, my company could provide it because we've built the infrastructure for it from the bottom up.

Implementing an improved elderly care solution and deploying strategically placed dialysis centers is also a need that I visualized being implemented throughout the Caribbean. Setting these tasks as goals and seeing them come to fruition would certainly bring me full circle in my life. This has been a personal mission for me; it is a part of my legacy. It would allow me to fulfill my purpose, my destiny, to carry on the dreams of those people on whose shoulders I'm standing. To bring their hopes and dreams to fruition is what I am about. This is what I tried to find when I left St. Kitts and Anguilla, and I now recognize that the answers were all right where I grew up. I just wanted to figure out how to help take care of the entire population. It's the same goal that we're trying to accomplish here in the United States: to adequately take care of the entire population. *My goal is, and has always been, to improve health care. I want to reclaim the patient-physician relationship, while also helping to empower physicians.*

The future of medicine should involve a more robust response to impending global epidemics and pandemics. It will mirror our human immune response of antigen recognition by T lymphocytes coupled with B cell diversity and antibodies. This is what it should look like:

Step 1. Early detection: A digital immune system should involve constant surveillance for disease frequency clearly in excess of normal expectancy. We should monitor sampling of blood, urine, and feces of humans as well as animals, including birds and arthropods.

Step 2. Sounding the alarm: If the threat of an outbreak is identified, this information should be relayed instantly to a "disease surveillance command center." As social media demonstrates, we already have the tools to accomplish this.

Step 3. Rapid response: Teams similar to hospital code teams or rapid-response teams of health providers that respond to hospitalized patients with early signs of clinical deterioration to prevent respiratory or cardiac arrest can be mobilized for potential outbreak emergencies. This team would need to be mobilized with the precision of a quick reaction force, a military unit of fifteen to thirty personnel capable of a rapid response to developing situations. Personnel and equipment should be ready to respond to any type of impending epidemic emergency within ninety minutes. If necessary, a larger rapid deployment force capable of a larger footprint similar to the military's special op, paratroopers, or marines could soon follow.

Step 4. Strict isolation/complete quarantine: The public should be protected by preventing exposure to hosts or potential hosts who have or may have a contagious disease during the period of communicability.

Step 5. Treat/repair: At this point, all the tools of modern medicine should be brought to bear, i.e. supportive medical care, antibiotics, antiviral medication, vaccine administration, development of new vaccines, insecticides if appropriate, etc. The disease attack rate and secondary attack rate should also be monitored closely, and the medical response should easily adapt to any changes in the threat.

Step 6. Augmentation: It may be necessary to augment the medical teams with reserve medical forces or reinforcements. This means that additional pre-organized personnel should operate on an "on-call" basis. The main role of the medical reserves would be to maintain fully trained status and to be available to deploy when needed to defend against the invasion of microbes.

Step 7. Debrief: What are the lessons learned? How can we better prepare for the next threat? Staying vigilant is key to our survival.

The journey of my life from childhood to owning multiple private practices has developed in me a drive to succeed and the realization that life is not solely about me but also about the lives on which I can have an impact. My story serves as an example or case study of how all those with a little determination can (1) lean on their own personal legacy and be inspired, (2) study the landscape or industry they are interested in so that they can navigate and have a complete understanding of what is required, and (3) use their own individual, innovative power and technology to discover and develop a formula for the best way forward.

PEARL #8:
By helping others, you invariably help yourself. It's not about money but about service.

CONCLUSION

*I have learned that success is to be measured not so much
by the position that one has reached in life as by the obstacles
which he has had to overcome while trying to succeed.*
—Booker T. Washington

And so here we are. This business model could now serve as a building block for the next level. It could serve as an executive summary for a strategic plan of expansion. We experienced our market-analysis summary, improved facilities, launched new services, streamlined operations, tested our SWOT analysis, proved our competitive advantage, formed our strategic alliances, tested our sales and marketing strategies, and balanced our books. Our team is now ready for the "long game," ready for investment analysis and offerings.

THE BENEFITS OF JOINING OUR TEAM ARE:

FINANCIAL BENEFITS:

1. Increased reimbursements for quality care

2. Reduced billing and collection leakage

3. Cost savings for group purchasing

4. Increased profitable volumes

5. Strengthened referral streams

6. Right-sized office and enhanced space

7. Audit, metrics, data stratification, and annual review guidance

8. Awareness for patients and beneficiaries

9. Navigation of available resources for high-risk patients

10. Local advocacy

CLINICAL BENEFITS:

1. Support for population health management, CCM, and TCM

2. Support for health IT, technology, infrastructure, and professional staff

3. Support for government/payer mandates

4. Improved patient outcomes

5. Practice and patient support for policies and processes, plus boots-on-the-ground support

6. Performance management

7. Access to the national leadership in practice-transformation efforts

8. Continuity of care integration

9. Work flow, cultural competency, and sensitivity training

10. Practice transformation, readiness survey, and coaching

PERSONAL BENEFITS:

1. Maintenance of practice autonomy and ownership

2. Alignment with top-performing colleagues (strength in numbers)

3. Reduced financial risk

4. Succession/retirement planning

5. Financial planning

6. Guidance on emergency funding

7. Knowledge to leverage assets

8. Diversification

9. Guidance in understanding the law, tax code, and implications

10. Less stress and greater life satisfaction

PATIENT BENEFITS THROUGH ELECTRONIC MEDICAL RECORDS AND ONLINE PATIENT PORTALS:

1. Access to lab results

2. Ability to request prescription refills

3. Ability to schedule appointments online

4. Ability to send and receive secure messages with the provider

5. Patient check in for appointments in advance

6. Reminders on important overdue tests

7. Ability to view billing history and pay remotely

8. Ability to receive alerts and updates from providers

CURRENT ALTERNATIVES TO PRIMARY CARE (I.E., "THE COMPETITION"—THIS IS WHY WE NEED TO UNITE AS INDEPENDENT PHYSICIANS):

1. Minute clinics (e.g., CVS minute clinic)

2. Urgent-care centers

3. Hospital investment in development of outpatient centers, shifting from inpatient to outpatient care

4. Employed physicians, nurse practitioners, and physician assistants

5. Alternative medicine providers

6. Escalating globalization

If traditional medicine and providing the highest quality of health care is for you, if you are *determined to practice*, then come and join our team.

PEARL #9:
Growth is a choice. Choose to think big.

Printed in the USA
CPSIA information can be obtained
at www.ICGtesting.com
JSHW012034140824
68134JS00033B/3061